Parents at Their Best

Dr. Clyde M. Narramore

Thomas Nelson Publishers
Nashville • Camden • New York

Copyright © 1985 by Clyde M. Narramore

Published in Nashville, Tennessee, by Thomas Nelson, Inc. and distributed in Canada by Lawson Falle, Ltd., Cambridge, Ontario.

Printed in the United States of America.

Scripture quotations are from THE NEW KING JAMES VERSION. Copyright © 1979, 1980, 1982, Thomas Nelson, Inc., Publishers.

Library of Congress Cataloging-in-Publication Data

Narramore, Clyde M. (Clyde Maurice), 1916-
  Parents at their best.

  1. Family—Religious life. 2. Parenting—Religious
aspects—Christianity. I. Title.
BV4526.2.N37   1985   248.4   85-21389
ISBN 0-8407-5426-4

Contents

The personal letters scattered throughout this book are composites of the wide variety of letters that I have received over the years. They represent the sorts of letters that I receive almost every day in my ministry and are not to be taken as representing any one person's problems.

CHAPTER
1

It's Getting Tougher

As I was putting some finishing touches on this book, I received an urgent phone call from a woman who pleaded with me to have an interview with her mother and father and her younger brother and sister.

"Our whole family has serious problems," she said. "I've gotten professional help myself, so I'm better, but everyone in the family has terrible hang-ups."

She hesitated for a moment before adding, "In a puny way, we all know the Lord. But I don't think my parents have any idea what they've done to create the problems in our home."

A few days later the family arrived in my office—the mother, the father, the daughter, eighteen, and the son, sixteen.

The girl had just been expelled from college, because, according to her parents, she had "gone wild" and had taken up with a bad crowd.

The boy was fighting with his parents, skipping classes, and running with a gang that was strong on drugs.

The parents were miles apart in their thinking.

As the weeks went on, we were able to offer Christ-centered professional counseling to each member of the family, and now they are achieving a reasonably good measure of adjustment.

Today in America, and indeed, in many countries, families like this are falling apart. And when this foundation crumbles, everything in society goes with it.

The home is the heart of society. It is where everything begins—ideas, attitudes, beliefs, and feelings. What happens in the family determines what takes place in the church, the school, the community, and the nation. A stable home provides children a solid basis from which to approach life. But an unstable home predisposes a child to a host of lifetime problems.

A secular atmosphere in which people question anything Christian pervades today's world. Most people live as they want to live, not as God wants them to. This attitude is affecting families. Our society is producing unhappy, non-spiritual people who are unable to establish godly homes.

About a week after graduating from college, a young man who was visiting our headquarters in California came into my office and said, "Doc, can I ask you about something?"

So we sat down and talked privately for a while.

"I'm saved, and all of that," he said, "but I don't know...I don't have much spiritual power. I've been dating a girl for about three weeks, and I don't know whether I ought to get her to go to bed with me or not."

We talked about his way of living; one statement seemed to sum it up: "Everything at college, on TV, and in society weakens me. It's that way, isn't it?"

How right he was.

The very first family had more than its share of problems. Adam and Eve had a son, Cain, who killed his brother, Abel. We have the account of this first family murder in Genesis 4:8-9:

> Now Cain talked with Abel his brother; and it came to pass, when they were in the field, that Cain rose against Abel his brother and killed him. Then the LORD said to Cain, "Where

is Abel your brother?" And he said, "I do not know. Am I my brother's keeper?"

Not only did Cain kill his brother Abel, he lied about it and disclaimed any responsibility for his own flesh and blood. Since then there's been trouble in the family, and the family has been in trouble!

We know that family problems will continue; we learn from the Word of God that in the last days before Christ comes again, times will get worse. The family problems today were predicted long ago.

> But know this, that in the last days perilous times will come: For men will be lovers of themselves, lovers of money, boasters, proud, blasphemers, disobedient to parents, unthankful, unholy, unloving, unforgiving, slanderers, without self-control, brutal, despisers of good (2 Tim. 3:1-3).

The more secular and godless a society becomes, the more trouble it heaps upon itself. When we leave God out of our homes, schools, courts of law, places of recreation, houses of worship, offices, industrial plants, and legislative bodies, we suffer the inevitable consequences, and the family seems hardest hit.

A woman who had recently given her heart to Christ called me, frantic about her son. "Dr. Narramore," she pleaded, "you've got to help my son. He has had a terribly disappointing experience. He's likely to commit suicide if we don't do something immediately. Will you phone him and do what you can for him? Try to lead him to Christ. He needs to be saved."

I agreed to phone him. We talked for almost an hour, and he told me about his life. His parents had been divorced when he was much younger. His family was quite wealthy, and he had attended a "prestigious" college. There he met a girl who was an "intellectual" and as sinful as himself. They moved in together and began a life of fornication. This relationship lasted for almost four years. Then suddenly, she met another boy she liked more, and she moved in with the new fellow. The young man I was counseling was devastated.

After he presented the details of this experience, I introduced the fact that he needed the Savior. But he couldn't understand what he needed to be "saved" from. When I mentioned sin, he said he didn't think of himself as a sinner. In fact, the whole idea of sinfulness was foreign and repulsive to him. He had been raised in a non-Christian home, had attended a non-Christian high school, and had graduated from a university that ridiculed Christianity. He was secularly brainwashed—no sin, no personal God, no need to change. All he needed, he thought, was something to keep him from coming unglued and committing suicide, but he had no idea what that "something" was.

This young man is representative of what happens to people who have been mesmerized by a secular, humanistic society, and who have not had the benefit of Christian parents to guide them toward a spiritually fulfilled life. As adults they suffer the consequences.

But you and I don't have to succumb to humanistic trends. If we forsake our sins and turn to Christ, He will honor and bless us. Trouble in our families will decrease, God said.

> Let the wicked forsake his way,
> And the unrighteous man his thoughts;
> Let him return to the LORD,
> And He will have mercy on him;
> And to our God,
> For He will abundantly pardon (Isa. 55:7).

The responsibility God gives to parents is both awesome

and wonderful. There is no greater joy than being a father or a mother, shaping the lives of human beings whom God has entrusted to their care.

My years of counseling with families have deepened my own awareness of the multitudes of family problems. Throughout this book I will discuss some of these potential problems and how they may be averted and/or solved. I have developed some guidelines that deal with such things as why children get into trouble, how to tell if a person needs professional help, and how to help your family become emotionally healthy.

Some parents have given up. Whatever they've done hasn't worked. They feel that they can't fight modern trends, so they cave in to present pressures. In fact, a couple recently said to me, "We're not planning to have any children. World conditions are too bad—drugs, alcohol, sex, violence, turmoil."

But we cannot afford to let these forecasters of doom and gloom dominate our thinking. *Today, families can be better and happier than ever.* God says,

> "All your children shall be taught by the LORD,
> And great shall be the peace of your children" (Isa. 54:13).

There is no logical way to twist or misinterpret God's clear and holy promise:

> If My people who are called by My name will humble themselves, and pray and seek My face, and turn from their wicked ways, then I will hear from heaven, and will forgive their sin and heal their land (2 Chron. 7:14).

God is in the blessing business. He created Adam and Eve, our forebears, not as slaves, but as companions. He loved them, protected them, provided for them, and talked with them. They were His own, and He loved them as He loves you and me today—beyond all human comprehension.

The home is the heart of society, and as parents, we can preserve the health of that vital organ. But first, let's take a look at what makes a family healthy and how to maintain that quality.

2

The Healthy Family

The healthy family is more than a group of people who simply live together and share experiences. When I say that the Smith family is a healthy one, I am not referring to the fact that each member is free from disease. I mean that each person, young or old, is enjoying life and becoming the person God intends him to be.

What are the characteristics of a healthy family? What goes on inside a home in which each person is living and developing in a healthy manner? Here, I believe, are some of the essences of a healthy family.

1. Developing Respect

In a healthy family, both parents and children develop respect for each other. The husband treats his wife with kindness and love, giving his family an example to follow.

To develop respect, parents need to listen carefully to children. Parents should not interrupt children when they are speaking. Not only does interrupting children frustrate them, but it also tells them that they are not significant persons. Parents should ask children for their suggestions. When they see their parents following through on some of those suggestions, they feel valuable as persons.

Another way for parents to show children respect is to encourage them to make their own decisions when possible. By being allowed to make some decisions, they learn that parents trust them and their judgment. This builds self-respect.

It is so important in building respect to be courteous to children. If parents say, "Thank you," "May I?" and "Please" to children, children will start using these phrases with others. Respect begets respect.

A child needs to hear positive comments about himself. We cause a child to be disrespectful when we continually tease him. He begins to feel inadequate and inferior.

To build respect, parents should take an interest in a child's activities. A child's school drawing is just as important to him as a big business deal is to a parent.

If you admit to your children that you are wrong when you *are* wrong, you cause them to respect you and to respect themselves when they make errors. Sometimes a parent will give a child a message to relay: "Tell them I'm not home," or "Tell them I can't, I'm sick." When these messages aren't true and the children know it, they lose respect for the parent. They also wonder if the parent may lie to them. This is one instance when a parent should admit to being wrong.

2. Discovering and Developing Talents

Every human being comes into this world with a unique set of talents and abilities, and the home is where each person's abilities and talents should be discovered, recognized, and developed. This is one of the most exciting and joyful parts of healthy family living! The family becomes stronger and benefits from having each individual developing and using his or her ability.

The family should encourage the mother in her interests and talents. The family should do the same for the father. No parent should be standing still. Each should be growing in talents. Each member of the family should encourage the father; each member of the family should encourage the mother. In this way they will both become happier, healthier, and more useful Christians.

Parents should discover the talents God has given each son and daughter. They should start looking for these interests at an early age. Although children change their interests from time to time while they are growing up, several talents usually persist throughout the childhood years, the teen years, and the adult years.

In a healthy family, parents do all they can to help each child discover his talents and use them in leisure time and in hobbies. Jimmy started showing an interest in photography around the age of nine. His parents encouraged him to read books and magazines on the subject. They bought him a simple camera so that he could take photographs, and they encouraged him in his picture taking. Jimmy really enjoyed this hobby and benefited from his parents' support.

3. Expressing and Showing Love

One of the most important emotional needs is love and affection. Every person has a longing for it; every person needs it. The best place to show, grow, develop, and exercise love and affection is in the home. By doing so, each member—mother, dad, son, and daughter—develops in a healthy manner and sidesteps many problems in life.

The giving and receiving of love and affection should apply to everyone in the family. Parents should show love to each other. Children should show love to parents, and parents should show love to their children. Brothers and sisters should love each other.

When this happens, each member of the family—but especially the child—will grow to respect himself and have healthy feelings toward himself. It will also establish trust and respect between members. When the child becomes an adult, his experience in a loving home will enable him to open himself to other people and be a blessing to them.

It's important for parents to remember to express their love verbally, accompanying their deeds. Actions are important, but words are reassuring. Parents should openly tell their child, "I love you, Billy" or "I love you, Cindy." As love is spoken in the home, children will grow up to love a husband or wife unreservedly. They will avoid the handicap of not being able to show and accept love.

4. Respecting Reasonable Limits and Boundaries

All life exists within boundaries. There are dos and don'ts for everyone in the world, whether we like it or not. The best place to learn to obey and regard these limits is in the home.

Parents in a healthy family present themselves as a model for their children by respecting the laws of the city, county, and nation. This respect is shown by both words and actions. Children learn to respect and like themselves better when they, like their parents, are obedient.

When a person breaks the law, he is disciplined by the justice system. So it is when children are disobedient; they must be disciplined. When parents discipline their children, they are showing that they love their children enough to make them obey. Some people have difficulty accepting this principle, but it's true nonetheless. The book of Proverbs states, "For whom the LORD loves He corrects,/Just as a father the son in whom he delights" (Prov. 3:12).

If a five-year-old boy insists on playing in the middle of a busy street and the only way to prevent his doing that is to punish him, then he must be punished. It isn't reasonable for a loving parent to allow his child to do something so foolish as to play in traffic.

Of course, correction and discipline should be appropriate for the child's age and personality. As a child grows older, parents should reason with him or her more and more rather than using corporal punishment. Some forms of punishment are more effective with certain children than others.

In teaching respect for law and exercising discipline, parents need to explain to the child why he must do what he must do or why he must be disciplined for his wrongs. Saying "do it because I told you to" does not help a child to either understand or respect authority.

5. Developing Healthy Self-images

Few things are more important to a child or an adult than a healthy self-image. A person's self-esteem carries him over many rough places in life.

Parents need to help their children develop positive feelings about themselves. A child with a good self-image is not only a joy to be around, but he will take that self-esteem into adulthood. Positive feelings about himself will enable him to adjust and adapt to changing situations.

Parents can build healthy self-images in their children by encouraging them to tell how they feel. Listening to children not only tells them they are important, but it also keeps the parents in touch with what's happening inside the children, how their personalities and characters are being formed and influenced.

Parents can show children that they are important to God. Teach them from the Bible that God Himself created them in His own image and that He saved them with a great price, the blood of His Son. Let the children know that angels are protecting them and that heaven has been prepared for them. All of these wonderful truths reassure children that they are not worthless. Their lives have value to God, and that should make life important to them.

But children aren't the only ones who benefit from healthy self-images. Parents do, too. So husbands and wives should be encouraging each other. No parent should have to go through a day without being recognized and encouraged by his or her mate.

6. Sensing the Community and World

In a healthy family children grow up realizing that they are not only a part of a family but also a part of the community and of nations beyond their own national borders. The days have passed when we could think only of ourselves. Hardly anything can happen in one country without another country being affected. Children should become aware of their responsibility for knowing what is happening to their fellow human beings.

In the Christian home, children should learn that their responsibility to the world goes beyond mere knowledge. It extends to finding ways in which they can help. Reaching down into their pockets for money for gifts to send those overseas who may be less fortunate is a concrete example that children can understand.

Unfortunately, in most homes children never have the opportunity to share in this way. Children grow up thinking about themselves, their own cars, their own possessions, or whatever. Thinking about other people in the community and in other countries, praying for them, and helping them have never been parts of their experience.

It's up to the parents to help each other and their children develop a world view. No family should curl up within itself and live like snails. Parents should be an example of being interested and caring about people or organizations around the world.

7. Becoming Spiritually Fulfilled

The healthy family is one that cares for all three areas of human life: physical, emotional, and spiritual. Many families neglect their spiritual needs, especially in their children.

Children, like adults, are spiritual beings. They have souls that must be fed or they will be dwarfed. Just as their bodies must be fed and clothed, so their spiritual natures must be nourished and cared for.

Once while traveling on a plane I sat alongside a businessman who told me about his family. He was very proud of his son who was a fine athlete. This man said that he had made it a point to encourage his children in school work and sports. He was sending them to one of the best (and most expensive) colleges in the nation so that they could make the most of their lives. When I asked him if he had met the children's spiritual needs, he looked at me as though I had just arrived from outer space. He was not a Christian, and he never thought about bringing God into his family.

As husbands and wives we should encourage each other to be at our best for Christ. No father, no mother should remain spiritually stagnant. We should help each other to grow.

As parents, we must ask ourselves if we have given our children eternal values. Have we done everything possible to develop their faith in God? We can help our children spiritually in a number of ways. To begin with, we can be examples of godliness; we can lead righteous lives that please God and give our children living examples to emulate. We can declare our trust in Jesus Christ and tell our children what Christ does in our lives.

The greatest joy, of course, is to lead children to the Lord, but spiritual care doesn't stop there. Parents can teach children to love and depend on God and to study the Bible. Parents can talk with their children about the Lord and help them interpret current events in light of God's Word and His plan for the world. Christian education is very important. With so many outstanding elementary and secondary schools, and with so many remarkably fine colleges, no child has to have an ordinary education. Meeting a child's spiritual needs determines where he will spend all eternity.

8. Identifying Personal and Family Goals

Just as an individual needs goals, so must each family have them. In a healthy family, parents encourage each other to achieve their goals. They support their children in making goals and in reaching them. Sadly, many children grow up without having any goals at all, and consequently, they have no direction for their lives.

Children need to understand the family's goals as well and should contribute toward them. Parents can discuss family goals with children during family get-together meetings and devotions.

In a healthy family each individual is interested in not only his own goals but also those of other family members. Everyone works to help the others achieve their aspirations.

Unfortunately, too many children grow up in homes where they eat meals, go to school, go to sleep, and repeat the same motions the next day. They stumble through life without definite goals. With only one life to live it's important to know which way to go and how to get there.

9. Working and Playing Together

One of the joys of healthy family living is working and playing together. In these modern times it's easy for the son to run to Little League, the daughter to Girl Scouts, mom to her club, and dad to his business meeting. As they are doing so, however, they are running away from one of the greatest joys of life—working and playing together as a family.

When we as parents spend time with our children, we're telling them that we love them. After all, we like to spend time with the people we love best and that should be our family. In a healthy family unit each person spends much of his leisure and fun time with other family members.

10. *Observing Good Health Habits*

It's hard for someone to act well unless he feels well. Parents have a responsibility to make sure that family members are in the best health possible and that everyone observes good health habits and feels fit. Parents do a lifetime of good for a child when they encourage him to observe good health habits and they take him for physical checkups.

As a psychologist working with parents and children through the years, I have been amazed at the number of adults who have told me that no one realized they had a hearing loss or a vision problem until they were nearly grown. One female physician told me, "I never knew that people didn't see double until I was in medical school." She went on to say that because she had two eyes, she assumed it was natural to see two of everything. For example, when a child stood in front of her, she saw two images of the same child.

About ten times a year various adult groups come to the campus of the Narramore Christian Foundation in Rosemead, California, for one or two weeks of specialized evaluation and training. During those times my staff and I come to know the people unusually well. A fact which never ceases to amaze me is that in each group of fifty to one hundred, we always identify several men and women who have rather serious physiological disorders. And, of course, these "body problems" are preventing their being as successful and well adjusted as they should be. How have such physical problems gone undetected for thirty or forty years? I'm sure that part of the answer lies in the fact that their parents had not observed them very carefully. In a healthy family, attention is given to each person's physical well being.

11. Meeting Mutual Financial Needs

In a healthy family, each person is interested in meeting the basic financial needs of the others. Children and parents should talk over the family budget and discuss what the family needs, what it can afford, and what it can't. In this way children can develop a practical mind for finances and a knowledge about earning and saving money. Parents can make a lifetime contribution to their children's welfare by helping them understand work, income, saving, and investing. Children need to develop sound, realistic attitudes toward money, although they should be aware that money is far from the most important thing in life.

Of course, one of the most important aspects of finances is tithing. What an advantage it is to a couple to begin their life together knowing that God has provided all that they have and all they ever will have! They learned from their parents the blessing of giving to Christian organizations. Now they carry that giving heart into their new life. Perhaps the biggest problem most Americans have with money is not their ability to earn it, but their attitude toward it. And this should be learned in the family.

12. Assuming Responsibilities in the Home

Each person is born to do—to work, to exercise, and to accomplish. It is a healthy family indeed that makes sure each member pulls his share and learns to accept responsibility at an early age. Of course, a child's responsibilities need to be in relation to his maturity, but every child can do something no matter how small he is.

Not long ago I spoke with a woman who was raised in a home where she never had any special responsibilities. "My mother was a perfectionist," she said. "I could never do anything to please her, so she would always shoo me out of the kitchen or wherever she was working, saying she'd do things herself. Of course, Mother could do things faster and better, but the tragedy was that when I got married, I couldn't do anything. I didn't know anything about running a house; and even worse, I didn't believe I was capable of doing it."

What a tragedy to send a child away to college or into marriage with the idea that he's limited in what he can do! When a person has learned to assume responsibilities and do jobs in the family, he feels more confident and has a healthier attitude toward himself.

If you are sincerely interested in evaluating your family and home life, you may want to mark the following chart. In this way you can identify areas you would like to improve. You may want to discuss these areas with your spouse and then make a definite effort to bring about changes.

You may also use the chart to consider what went on in your own childhood as you were growing up. As you discuss these areas with another person, you may come to a better understanding of why you feel and act the way you do. This procedure can then become the basis for change.

Unfortunately, too many families today neglect one or more of these important elements. When that happens, the family suffers. Parents must do their best to remedy this situation and lead their family to a fuller, healthier life in accordance with God's will.

THE HEALTHY FAMILY

	Good	Average	Poor
1. Developing Respect			
2. Discovering and Developing Talents			
3. Expressing and Showing Love			
4. Respecting Reasonable Limits and Boundaries			
5. Developing Healthy Self-images			
6. Sensing the Community and World			
7. Becoming Spiritually Fulfilled			
8. Identifying Personal and Family Goals			
9. Working and Playing Together			
10. Observing Good Health Habits			
11. Meeting Mutual Financial Needs			
12. Assuming Responsibilites in the Home			

CHAPTER

3

An Image Restored

In the summer of 1984 my family and I took a tour group on a Greek Island cruise. We were eager to see Patmos where the apostle John was exiled and where he wrote the book of the Revelation. We were also looking forward to seeing Mars Hill in Athens where Paul gave his favorite address.

You can imagine our excitement when we boarded the beautiful liner in Athens to begin our cruise. As we stepped on the ship we were handed a specially printed greeting. It read:

> Sail away!
> Break away!
> Forget all your worries, and the ship will carry you through the temples of magic and mystery...to the islands of freedom! Days of pleasure, fun, relaxation, and excitement! Days that can change your outlook on life!

My, I thought, *this is going to do more for me than I expected*! But as we sailed from one island to the other and returned to our home port of Athens, I found that the cruise didn't really bring that much change. Many of the passengers used the cruise as an attempt to escape their problems. Some were drinking, some were gambling, and some were living in immorality. As I walked around the decks, I met various passengers whose lives were plagued with severe problems. A boat ride wasn't going to produce a big change for them.

So it is with most activities that people are scrambling in and out of. People hold high hopes, but they are soon let down. However, there is a really big change that can turn a person completely around, giving him a new nature and making him wonderfully different. The gift of eternal life, available to all, creates a new nature within a person enabling him to live righteously. People will not be let down when they accept this gift.

Need for a Change

Why do we need this big change? Why do we need a new nature? After all, we are masterpieces of God's creative efforts, aren't we? In fact, we are gifted above all other creatures, but we are also burdened by a thing called "sin." Let's look more closely at this issue in order to answer these questions.

"In the image of God He made man" (Gen. 9:6). There is no question about the unique position of superiority this image and likeness have given humans in relationship to other creatures. The heavenly Father created man to "have dominion" over all the other creatures (Gen. 1:26).

Man is the "image and the glory of God" (1 Cor. 11:7). Many parts of holy Scripture proclaim man's special place in creation:

You have made him a little lower than the angels,
And You have crowned him with glory and honor.
You have made him to have dominion over the works of Your
   hands;
You have put all things under his feet (Ps. 8:5–6).

A well-known event just before the Flood took place aptly illustrates the unique intelligence of humans. Before entering the ark, Noah was given the complicated instructions to take two of certain kinds of animals (a male and a female) and seven each of other kinds. Only a human being would have had the intelligence to follow such instructions.

Another example of man's unique intellectual ability is referred to in Genesis 2:19–20. Adam gave names to all the creatures. What creature could accomplish such a feat? Human beings certainly possess a quality and degree of intelligence and talent beyond any other beings in God's great creation.

Man's high intelligence and giftedness are only a part of his total personality. Another aspect is his tendency to sin, which became evident when the first man and woman, Adam and Eve, were placed in the Garden of Eden. "Then the LORD God took the man and put him in the garden of Eden to tend and keep it. And the LORD God commanded the man, saying, 'Of every tree of the garden you may freely eat; but of the tree of the knowledge of good and evil you shall not eat, for in the day that you eat of it you shall surely die' " (Gen. 2:15–17). But Adam and Eve did not do as they were told: "So when the woman saw that the tree was good for food, that it was pleasant to the eyes, and a tree desirable to make one wise, she took of its fruit and ate. She also gave to her husband with her, and he ate" (Gen. 3:6). When this happened, God took action: "Therefore the LORD God sent him out of the garden of Eden to till the ground from which he was taken" (Gen. 3:23).

A Universal Need

When our parents, Adam and Eve, sinned in the Garden of Eden, they were driven out, and a curse came upon all mankind. Man was separated from God. His sinful nature was transmitted to all human beings who would ever come upon earth: "Therefore, just as through one man sin entered the world, and death through sin, and thus death spread to all men, because all sinned" (Rom. 5:12).

Unfortunately, the superior potential of man did not bring him to God; rather it enticed him away. "The world through wisdom did not know God" (1 Cor. 1:21). Romans 1:22 states that "professing to be wise, they became fools." A blanket of condemnation fell over all the human race: "For all have sinned and fall short of the glory of God" (Rom. 3:23).

The tendency to do evil is universal. It's a part of all races in all places. As certain elements within our country are attempting to purge spiritual essentials of Christianity from public schools and other institutions, crime and violence increase. On the international level, evil men are forcing one nation after another into godless communism.

It's not necessary, of course, to look only to criminals and Communists to find sin. Unregenerate man has a complete lack of drive or motivation toward God. The Lord made the following assessment of human beings: they are "dead in trespasses and sins" (Eph. 2:1).

Humans with all their God-given abilities are in a sorry state. Each generation fails to make people better. All the progress in the world doesn't change the nature of man, and as a counseling psychologist, I am faced with this fact every day. They "commit the abominations" and fill "the land with violence" (Ezek. 8:17) because of their evil nature. God "saw that the wickedness of man was great in the earth, and that every intent of the thoughts of his heart was only evil continually" (Gen. 6:5). He needed a regeneration that would change the sinful tendencies of his human nature.

How is it possible for humans to possess the potential for fellowship with God and with Satan at the same time? How can they be talented and intelligent, yet sinful and violent? The answer lies in the dual nature within humans. This wonderful product of God's perfect creation enables them to sing beautiful songs, write lovely poems, run amazing races, and build graceful buildings. But at the same time, they are imperfect and unable to stand righteously in the presence of a holy God. Indeed, since the Garden of Eden, they have possessed wonderful qualities and great potential along with their sinful natures.

That's why the Lord Jesus left the wonders of heaven to suffer and die on the cross for us. He made it possible for us to be born again and leave behind the "old man." We receive our spiritual nature, and each of us becomes a "new man," according to the Word of God.

The New Nature

Without this new nature it is impossible to please God (see Rom. 8:8). Without this new nature even the good things we do are unacceptable to Him. Isaiah 64:6 reminds us that "all our righteousnesses are like filthy rags." We can do nothing on our own to change this sinful nature: "But without faith it is impossible to please Him, for he who comes to God must believe that He is, and that He is a rewarder of those who diligently seek Him" (Heb. 11:6).

Listen to the experience of the apostle Paul who desperately endeavored to eliminate his bad habits: "For what I am doing, I do not understand. For what I will to do, that I do not practice; but what I hate, that I do....For I know that in me (that is, in my flesh) nothing good dwells; for to will is present with me, but how to perform what is good I do not find" (Rom. 7:15, 18). During the almost two thousand years since then, countless thousands have experienced the same failures.

An Old Testament prophet illustrated the truth this way: "Can the Ethopian change his skin or the leopard its spots?/

27

Then may you also do good who are accustomed to do evil" (Jer. 13:23). It simply is not possible for anyone to eliminate the roots of his own sinful nature.

How then can anyone live a clean, decent, and spiritually fulfilling moral life? The answer is spiritual salvation—becoming a new person in Christ Jesus. When this takes place, "old things have passed away" and "all things have become new" (2 Cor. 5:17).

A Scriptural Example

Before the apostle Paul's conversion he was full of hate. The Bible describes him as "breathing threats and murder" against Christians (Acts 9:1). He participated in the stoning to death of Stephen (see Acts 7-8). Then, in the very midst of a mission of hate and violence, he became converted to a saving faith in the Lord Jesus Christ. From that time on he was a changed person. He experienced the big change!

Spiritual conversion has taken place in multitudes of lives. Drunken abusers have been almost instantly transformed into affectionate parents. Hate and violence have changed into love and kindness. No good intentions for moral reformation can ever accomplish the changes brought about by the spiritual regeneration of God's great salvation. Regenerating grace will create not only a new spirit in the heart but also a new environment in the home. Parents who receive this new spirit will want to help their children receive it too.

When a human being accepts God's gift of salvation through faith in Christ Jesus, he is born anew spiritually. At that time an individual has the potential for achieving the full measure of happy, righteous living for which he was created. It is possible to live through one's new spiritual nature to the glory of God and to the benefit of society.

On several occasions I have spoken to the president's staff at the White House. During one of these sessions forty-two people were present. After a time of questions and answers about personal, family, and emotional problems, I brought a message, "The Greatest Thought That Can Enter the Human Mind." This, of course, has to do with the contemplation of eternal life through being born again spiritually. At the conclusion I said, "Today we're at the brain center of the whole world. You make many decisions, but the greatest decision you'll ever make is now before you: Will you confess your sin, invite Christ into your life, and be saved?"

Immediately eight of the forty-two raised their hands and said yes. They prayed and asked Christ to come into their hearts. Immediately they were given new natures—new capacities—and entered into eternal life!

Spiritual conversion is the ultimate change. It's not a weekend boat cruise! Nothing else produces such a thoroughgoing personal revolution. Why? Because at the moment of conversion, God's Holy Spirit invades the personality and remains there to do His work in the person's life. Words cannot adequately express the growth that comes as through the years, the born-again person yields himself to Christ, reads the Scriptures, and becomes conformed to the image of Christ. He isn't perfect, but he *is* changed and growing and becoming kind, honest, respectful, and loving. What a change!

I might add, too, that spiritual conversion meets all the requirements of the scientific method. Nothing has ever been put in the scientific test tube so often, in so many places, under every possible condition, with such diverse people of all ages, yet produced such persistent, consistent results!

So-called Christians

Non-Christians may question the validity of spiritual conversion. They look at a believer who has problems, and they wonder why he is behaving the way he is. "If he is saved," they ask, "why is he acting like that?"

This is a valid question, and I would like to offer some explanations. The person the unbeliever thinks is a Christian may not be one at all. Simply because a person goes to church, is vitally interested in the church, and is a member of a Christian family doesn't mean that he is a true Christian. There is a world of difference between a "religious" person and one who has been born anew by the Spirit of God. Consequently, that person who seems to be religious but is not given over to Christ is without real spiritual power and control in his life. He is in just as much need of God as though he had never heard of the Bible and had never been inside a church. The Bible speaks of such a person as one who has the appearance of godliness but denies its power (see 2 Tim. 3:5).

Naturally the unbelieving man or woman can't really tell the difference between a Christian person and a merely religious person. Since the unsaved onlooker does not have spiritual insight, he is spiritually blinded—they both may look the same to him.

Another reason that a so-called Christian may not be acting like one is because he is a member of a false cult. Such a cult may teach some basic doctrines of the Bible but omit others. As a result it masquerades as a fervently religious group. It is thought to be Christian in nature but in actuality is far from it.

Just last week after a luncheon a man asked me privately why a certain man would be committing incest with both his daughters. "I can't understand," he said, "why a person who is so religious would do such a thing."

I pointed out to him that the man in question was a member of a cult, and in that cult such behavior was not unusual. I tried to point out that the perpetrator wasn't a true Christian, but I didn't get very far because the questioner himself was an unbeliever and hardly knew what I was talking about.

The world is filled with people who belong to some cult or sect. Although they may be very religious, they do not know Christ as their personal Savior. Consequently, their moral behavior may be unaffected by their religious practices.

Another reason why a so-called Christian may not be living up to what he knows is that he may be a "baby" Christian. He may be barely saved or living a carnal life. Recently, I talked by phone to a man who has acknowledged Christ as his personal Savior, but he is miserable because he is living in sin. His conduct certainly is not consistent with his profession of faith.

As a psychologist, I frequently see born-again Christians whose behavior belies their professed beliefs. It's not uncommon for someone to have a physiological problem severely affecting his behavior. A medical problem, such as a neurological impairment, may be having a strong negative influence on him. Anyone suffering severe emotional deprivations from childhood may not seem to be saved. As adults, these people are sometimes paranoid, insecure, hostile, manipulative, or in some other way maladjusted. It's not easy to be spiritual if you have serious emotional hangups.

All of these problems—being unsaved, belonging to a cult, being carnal, or suffering from a physical or emotional disorder—can never destroy the fact that a human being can be truly born again by God's Holy Spirit. Such a person is indwelt by God's Holy Spirit, and he displays Christlike behavior. Millions can attest to it. Take a look at this letter I've recently received.

> Dear Dr. Narramore:
> I was severely abused as a child and young adult. I spent years in psychotherapy with some of the country's leading therapists. It was not until I prayed to God out of my darkness and pain and confusion did I find Hope and Light for my life. That Hope and Light was His Son Jesus Christ. Not only have I found *Peace, Joy and Happiness* in my daily life; I have found my salvation and faith.
> God has given me such faith and fullness thru His Son Jesus Christ that in the past few years I have been able to reach out of the "dark pit" in which I once lived to help others in a loving Christian way. God is currently enabling me to study for a Doctor's (Ph. D. degree in Psychology). I work with therapy groups—victims of child abuse, and with other mental disorders. I grow in love and forgiveness toward my family while guiding them to God and Christ.

A change in life is available through a personal relationship with Jesus Christ. This single most powerful source for changing our nature causes us to live productive, godly lives. When we experience this change, we will become more complete marriage partners, parents, friends, employees, and citizens. Our homes and our communities will be better for it, and they will develop in ways consistent with God's will.

CHAPTER
4

A Premarriage Checklist

One evening in a small counseling group, a man was talking about the many problems in his marriage. For some time he talked about how little he and his wife had in common. In fact, it was a real struggle for them to make the changes necessary for a "possible" marriage.

A woman in the group asked if he had known his wife very well before he married her.

"Oh, no," he shot back. "I was young and I just married her for her body."

Many people enter into marriage as this man did. They know very little about their mate before they sign the marriage contract. They have given little thought to the personality characteristics of the one with whom they think they want to spend the rest of their lives. In a sense, upon getting married many men and women are taking home a "pig in a poke"! They don't really know what they are getting.

Marriage decisions usually affect generations. First, of course, the couple is affected. Then, their children are affected and, in time, their grandchildren. Many people will benefit tremendously from a right decision, but many people will suffer grievously from a wrong decision.

Good parenting begins long before a child arrives in a family. It stems from dating, falling in love, and getting married. Good parents think long and hard about whom they date and whom they marry.

We undoubtedly have more knowledge about personality traits and their causes than ever before. If a person anticipating marriage will give careful consideration to understanding a potential mate, a lifetime of tragedy can be sidestepped. One simply doesn't have to marry the wrong person. It is possible to read the signs, pick up the clues, and know something of what to expect after saying, "I do."

I've compiled a checklist of ten vitally important areas that every person contemplating marriage should consider thoughtfully and thoroughly. Each point reveals desirable or undesirable traits that may affect the marriage's future. By seeing how these traits can bring trouble or success, you will become aware of these premarriage signals. Whether you're the person considering wedlock, a soon-to-be parent-in-law, grandparent-in-law, or friend-in-law, this list is worth your time and prayerful consideration.

1. Emotional Adjustment

It was a perfect wedding. The bride and groom made a handsome couple. All their friends and family were able to attend. Everything went just right throughout the ceremony and the reception.

This ideal state, however, ended abruptly. On the second morning of the honeymoon the bride, Jane, threw a temper tantrum. She wildly tossed things from her luggage. First a brush, then a cosmetic bottle, followed by her shoes and just about everything else she could get her hands on. Jane's wild behavior became even more disturbing to her new husband, Bob, as she raised her voice more loudly with each new outburst.

Bob could hardly believe his eyes and ears! He had never seen anything like it before. He was about ready to physically intervene before a window was smashed when just as suddenly as it had begun the outburst ceased.

What did I do to cause this? was all he could think of. Jane's only response was an unemotional, "Forget it."

Now, twenty years later, many similar episodes have all but extinguished the love they once felt for each other. What was the cause of her emotional outbursts? What made her act that way? Why hadn't he noticed any tendency toward such behavior during their months of courtship?

Problems in emotional adjustment are found in both men and women far too often to discount the importance of their critical considerations *before* the marriage vows are taken. Jane's problem was one of emotional instability. Infants are not born that way. They become so when certain basic emotional needs are not adequately met at critical stages of development. During the child's infancy and early years the parents—both of them—are the most significant fulfillers (or deprivers) of basic emotional needs that help assure healthy emotional adjustment in the growing young person.

In her teens, Jane had enough intelligence and self-control to maintain the general appearance of good adjustment in most social situations. Meanwhile, her boy friend Bob was too blinded by her physical attractiveness to notice much else. He should have paid more attention to Jane's emotional reactions to her parents, younger brother, and friends. He should have noticed how she handled disappointment, like the times he had to break a date. What were her reactions to being corrected or challenged? Bob should have made mental notes of how Jane accepted compliments or if she found it easy to criticize other people. By observing her behavior, he might have been able to pick up on her problems or maladjustments. If Bob had seen more of how his fiancée related to her family, he might have been able to keep her from bringing all of her insecurities and hostilities into the marriage.

2. *Goals*

"What are your goals?" Sharon asked her boy friend Tim.

To her great surprise he said, "I want to make a couple hundred thousand bucks as fast as I can and then retire, living off the interest."

"That was a serious question I asked you," complained Sharon.

Tim assured her that he had meant exactly what he said. "I want some fun out of life. I don't want to just get involved so deeply in making a living that there is no time for pleasure."

To some people, the only purpose in life is simply to have fun! Others follow various kinds of advice: "Never marry for love: look for a man with money"; "Get a good secure job with the government"; "Do better than your brother"; and so on.

Yet, as many divorced people will tell you, these kinds of goals don't guarantee everlasting happiness. It's possible, of course, to be overly idealistic in dedicating oneself to an altruistic or unrealistic goal in life. But it is important to have goals. It is dangerous for a person not to have them.

You may want to stop right now and ask yourself, *Do I know what I want to do with my life? What are my goals and aspirations?* Are you giving serious thought to your abilities and aptitudes? Or are you simply an "occupational drifter," taking whatever job comes along?

"Just what will help me to make the right choice?" Bob asked his vocational counselor at high school. They talked about his ambitions and his vocational test scores. Some of his scores were a real surprise to him. As time went on, Bob came to realize that the tests were quite accurate, and they were helpful to him.

Bob chose a good place to start collecting such information, but a Christian should not stop there. You will be in line for a totally fulfilling experience in life when you also seek spiritual direction to your planning. I don't mean you must be a minister or missionary, although that is a tremendous possibility. You should seek God's plan for your life with a dedicated willingness to completely follow that plan. Few things in this life will bring the personal satisfaction of accurately finding and obediently following the Lord's perfect will for your life.

> Only one life, 'twill soon be past;
> Only what's done for Christ will last.

What about your "intended"? Does he or she have specific goals? Do you know what they are? List them; talk about them. Compare them with yours. Are the two of you heading in a similar direction? Are your goals compatible? Are the goals desirable? Attainable? Is either of you being selfish in your goals? What about motivation?

Jill, a highly motivated young woman, married Don. In time she became exasperated with what she considered Don's lack of ambition and drive, and Don was fed up with Jill's impatience with him. Thirty years later the picture hadn't changed much. They had lived together, yet they hadn't. They had existed in the same house, but their goals had been and still were miles apart. How unfortunate that they never seriously considered this problem before they said, "I do."

I sometimes ponder what is going to happen when we all stand before God, giving account of what we have done the few years we were on earth. I'm afraid many Christians will realize that they have spent their time working at some job almost any unsaved person with the same ability could have done just as well. Meanwhile they could have been doing something that will count through all eternity. Couples will discover too late that while striving for that house on the hill, they lost focus of the needs in the valley. Others will know the pain of having a prodigal son because they felt having a second income was more important than someone staying home to raise the boy.

Think it over. Check your goals and those of the one you intend to marry. Ask yourself where God fits in.

3. Intelligence

Another aspect that should be considered before marriage is intellectual compatibility. In the first flush of love some young couples never give a thought to the important part the mind plays in complementing each other. Yet it has been observed that the amount of intelligence necessary to please us is an indication of the amount of intelligence we have ourselves.

To enjoy a creative and fulfilling life nothing is finer than the development of your intellectual powers. As an intelligent person yourself, you will not be satisfied in a marriage relationship with a partner whose capacity and interest are limited.

Anne married her "superman" knowing she would be hard put to measure up to his high expectations of her, but she figured it would work out. Years later, disillusioned, she told me, "If I had only known how far Ed and I were apart intellectually, I would never have married him. I have knocked myself out and suffered a nervous breakdown trying to keep pace."

When Alan became interested in a possible life-relationship with Donna, her broad intellectual interests and abilities were part of her appeal. He was impressed as he observed similar qualities in her brother and parents. He also noticed their thoughtfulness toward one another, their happy interpersonal relationships, and the rich spiritual tone of her family and home. After many years of a happy marriage, Alan and Donna have no doubts that God intended them for each other.

Another consideration in marrying an intelligent mate is that bright parents are much more likely to have bright children. What parent does not want his children to be able to learn quickly and well?

What heartache and disillusionment might be avoided if couples considered before marriage the value of a reasonable equality in their intellectual abilities and interests.

4. Education

Some young people in search of a life partner may overlook the importance of education and training. A man must have an adequate earning capacity in order to effectively assume the responsibility of a family. The Bible says, "But if anyone does not provide for his own, and especially for those of his household, he has denied the faith and is worse than an unbeliever" (1 Tim. 5:8).

The wise young man evaluates his talents and potential, then sets his goals. Next he pursues the education and training necessary to equip himself for a suitable career. He may then be considered a good prospect as a marriage partner.

The young woman is also enhanced by a good education. Each of the four qualities mentioned in 1 Timothy 5:14 which God desires of a Christian woman will be enriched by a trained mind; young women should "marry, bear children, manage the house, give no opportunity to the adversary to speak reproachfully."

It should be kept in mind that the well-educated husband

may outgrow his partner who has neither a good education nor the desire to improve herself. Their communication level will be poor. He may become bored listening to her, and she will be overwhelmed by the subjects he enjoys talking about. Love—that mysterious, misunderstood, but important part of life—is not all there is in marriage.

Jean was an intelligent, talented, ambitious woman. She fell in love with a handsome, intelligent man she met at church. Even though he had dropped out of high school to take a job with little or no future, she was sure she could "fire" him with the ambition he lacked. So they married. After several children were born, and after many frustrating events, he did attempt to continue his education, but not until many years and the chance for many happy family experiences had been lost forever. In all too many such marriages unhappiness and even divorce become the unfortunate fruits of inadequate education preparation.

In addition to considering educational compatibility, young people contemplating marriage would do well to consider the advantages of a better education. The earning power of the man or woman who is well educated may help attain those goals of better living conditions and financial security, to say nothing about giving larger gifts to the Lord's work or being more qualified to perform a certain ministry. A good education can open vistas for a greater appreciation of life in general and of one's family.

5. Vocation

The husband's vocation usually determines the family's life patterns. Certain factors should be taken into account:

- If his job takes him from home often or for long periods of time, the wife has to assume more than her share of responsibilities.

- If it's seasonal employment, the family finances will have to be planned accordingly.
- Job security is more reliable in some vocations than in others.
- Some companies require that their employees move from place to place every few years.
- Certain occupations sometimes place heavy social obligations upon the wife. Some women enjoy this, while others dislike it.

These and other factors should be considered before you seriously consider a lifemate. They do add up to happiness or unhappiness. Any bride-to-be who says, "I'm marrying him, not his job," should spend some serious time reflecting on the ramifications of the vocational aspects of family life. Likewise, a soon-to-be husband must decide if his chosen profession is going to create or allow the home life he desires.

David and Robin married while he was in the Air Force. The couple survived those early years while David finished his hitch. Now he's a civilian, working for the county fire department. Robin was happy to wait out the enlisted years, believing that when they were completed, she and David would be able to see more of each other. But the scheduled "ten days on, four days off" that the fire department requires doesn't mix with Robin's eight-to-five, five-days-a-week job. In evaluating their two jobs, David and Robin considered the pay, the benefits, and the future, but they overlooked the "now."

Another situation shows how complex this consideration of vocation can be. The young woman has vocational aspirations, but the young man she's interested in marrying tells her, "I want a homemaker, not a business partner." Can he guarantee that he will always be around to provide for his homemaker? No life insurance policy can provide the financial security and emotional satisfaction brought about by the young woman's credentials in an occupation that both rewards and challenges her.

Mary's problem was different. One of five children in a home where there was never enough money, she decided she would be a working wife so that she and her husband would have enough money for conveniences and some luxuries. But as time went on, she began to wish her husband would increase his earning capacity. She wanted to be able to look forward to having a comfortable home and a secure future without having to work so hard outside the home. She had never thought to look for such personal qualities in her boy friend before he became her husband.

A significant ingredient in the happiness of your future home will be the occupational satisfaction of your mate. The wife who comes home every night from a long, sometimes frustrating day at the office will not always be in a happy emotional condition. Husbands who spend year after year seated on a bench before a factory machine, performing tasks that bore them, may become irritable and displeased with life in general. Anyone who feels locked into an undesirable job situation will not be at his best—at home or at work. Couples should investigate their attitudes toward their chosen occupations and discuss them before the wedding, not after it.

6. Health

Young love so often overlooks the considerations of health hazards in the choice of a mate. But health and an able body are twin jewels that are beyond price.

A woman once said to me, "I knew John was sickly; I was aware of this before we got married. But I wanted to nurse him back to good health." She sighed as she continued, "But

I didn't know I'd be doing it for nineteen years!" She had gone into the marriage with her eyes open, but she hadn't realized that in signing the marriage contract she was virtually signing a "private hospital" agreement. In addition she had to work to provide for the family. She had been so insecure, so eager to get married for fear of being left out, that she was willing to marry almost anyone regardless of his state of health. It was a high price to pay, and it didn't work out for either of them.

Another girl, Edna, walked into a marriage in which both families had a history of asthma. Physicians pointed out to her that in such a case any children would have a strong propensity toward asthma, but Edna felt she couldn't live without her Charles. They married, and their two children—a boy and a girl—were both plagued with asthma. Edna's life was spent between the doctor's office and the drugstore, which added many pressures to an already shaky marriage.

If we were to look for a mate who was perfect in every respect, including health, no one would ever get married. Some of the finest individuals have physical handicaps which will place certain restrictions upon future family activities. These handicaps should not be overlooked, but neither should they be the sole criteria.

No family will go through life completely free from illness. Our unredeemed bodies will be vulnerable to disease and infirmity until "the redemption of our body" (Rom. 8:23). What we can do is prevent a double portion of such problems by marrying a healthy mate. What follows then—"in sickness or in health"—can be borne with grace and acceptance, not regret.

7. Talents

You may be asking what talent has to do with a happy

marriage. Let me illustrate. Bob and three other men were meeting at Bob's home for a quartet rehearsal. Their wives had come along and were chatting in another room. "Who'll play for us tonight?" one of the quartet asked. The bass spoke up, "My wife can play if you want her to." "My wife is a good pianist," the tenor chipped in. Bob said, "My wife's a good accompanist." The fourth singer looked thoughtful as he commented, "How come you three married such talented women? *My* wife can't do anything much." They laughed a bit, then the bass replied, "Well, Paul, I guess it was like this: we did some thinking before we got married!"

Actually there was a lot of truth in what he said. Some people do think before they get married, and an important thing to think about is what talents your spouse-to-be will be bringing to your marriage. Some marriages are pretty sparse in this area. Others are amazingly vital with tremendous talent. The choice is yours. What you choose is what you must live with for years and what will affect your children as well.

Have you ever wondered at the marvelous distribution of talents with which God has endowed mankind? "Each one has his own gift from God, one in this manner and another in that" (1 Cor. 7:7). Think of the skills needed for the maintenance of the quality of life we enjoy. Craftsmen, doctors, dentists, musicians, mechanics, scientists, educators, computer operators, and hundreds of others meet our daily needs. Sometimes many applicants apply for the same job, but rarely is there a skill requirement that cannot be filled by someone.

You will want to notice the extent to which your intended mate has developed his or her talents as well as how these talents are used. Jack, for example, appeared to have considerable potential for working effectively with boys, but he would never make the effort to teach a Sunday school class or to assist in youth activities. Almost all his free time was spent watching TV. Talents are of no value until they have been sufficiently developed and are being productively used.

It's not necessary for a wife and husband to have the same abilities. When two people become one in Christ, their diverse abilities should complement each other in such a way as to enrich their family life and their Christian testimony. At the same time their similar talents will bring them together in their activities and interests.

Bob, for instance, loved woodworking and had accumulated a fine set of tools. His wife, Esther, had other interests. She was creative in oil painting. In the workshop Bob built a special corner with places for Esther to practice her skills while he worked on his. They were both happy and content with each other.

Kay and Marvin, on the other hand, enjoyed their music together. She was a fine pianist and he sang well. They spent many happy evenings exercising these talents. In addition they had opportunities for Christian service.

Talents are gifts from God. A truly happy, fulfilling marriage relationship can be enhanced when these are developed and used.

8. Family Involvement

Many young people enter into marriage not realizing that it involves *three* families: (1) the newlyweds; (2) the wife's family; and (3) the husband's family. The young couple learns this all too soon.

"I didn't marry your mother," Ted angrily exclaimed to Mary. "I'm sick and tired of spending every Sunday with her."

Mary's heart was crushed as he spoke. She had been eager

to help her mother in the painful adjustment to life as a widow. That night Mary went to bed but not to sleep; her thoughts were on how she could please both her husband and her mother.

Ted's mother and father were always careful not to encroach upon the privacy of their son and daughter-in-law, and both families enjoyed their times together. But Mary's mother had a tendency to subtly suggest that "this or that" be changed in their home. Ted often rebelled at her continued interference. As Mary discussed the problem with her mother, it was decided to limit the Sundays spent at her house. Although Mary's mother felt hurt about the decision, this couple was taking a step in the right direction.

In another family, the son-in-law proudly said, "Dad is a benediction to our home. We love him and he loves us." This is the way it should be.

Unless you marry an orphan, you will have to deal with your spouse's parents. This does not mean you have to be as equally compatible with your mother-in-law as you are with your spouse, but it does mean having to understand her if possible. Don't assume that she will change, and don't plan on locking the door when you see her coming. If you feel the tension with prospective in-laws is too great, you may be wise to take a second look at your future in-laws. It may be best not to get tangled up in such a family. Or it might be wise to come to know them better and to declare your independence long before the wedding bells ring.

Happy, well-adjusted, and satisfied in-laws have a tremendous influence on a young couple. Unfortunately, the opposite is also true. Don't underestimate the potential of your "three family" relationships. They can enrich or cripple a marriage.

9. Friends

A person's friends can tell you a lot about that person. Not only does the type of friends reflect something about a future spouse, but so does the number of friends he or she has.

Have you ever known a person who did not have a good friend? Janis is that unfortunate kind of person. The other students at school seem to pay little attention to her. Whenever she tries to talk to people, they seem in a hurry to terminate the conversation. Even at church she is usually alone.

Why are some people this way? One reason Janis has become a social isolate outside the home is because she has always been one inside her home. Her older brother gets most of the attention. From the very beginning she has learned to defer to others. Since she has never learned appropriate reactions to attention, she acts silly whenever she receives polite consideration. This behavior, of course, only further aggravates her problem.

"As Christians, our business is people," Dr. Wallace Emerson, Christian psychologist, often reminded his students. He was right. Seldom does a social hermit accomplish much for the Lord. We are to witness to the unsaved; "he who wins souls is wise" (Prov. 11:30). We are to "visit orphans and widows in their trouble" (James 1:27). We are to "be hospitable to one another" (1 Pet. 4:9). Is the one with whom you are considering marriage capable and willing to establish with you that kind of home?

Now ask yourself, "What kind of friends does my mate-to-be have? Am I comfortable with these friends? Do they tend to be uplifting or discouraging? Do I want these people around my children?" These considerations are important to a successful marriage.

Rick was a socially gregarious young husband. He encouraged his many friends to wander in and out of his house at will. His wife liked people, but she wanted more family privacy. This conflict of domestic social interests rubbed both of them the wrong way. In time it contributed to the failure of the marriage.

The old adage, "You can tell a man by the company he keeps," is true. Men and women considering marriage need to examine their future spouse's friendships and see what they may say about that prospective partner's life.

10. Spirituality

"Do not be unequally yoked together with unbelievers. For what fellowship has righteousness with lawlessness? And what communion has light with darkness?" (2 Cor. 6:14). Have you ever wondered why God put this verse in the Bible? It's because He loves you and wants you to have a radiant, happy life. God has many laws. One of them is gravity. You can be sure that if you jump out of a seventh-story window, you'll go down, not up. So it is with God's law regarding marriage. If you disobey it, you'll suffer the consequences.

Christians are not to marry one who has never been born again in Christ Jesus. Why is this so important? What difference does it make? Because God says so just as plainly as He says, "You shall not steal" (Exod. 20:15). If you want to please the Lord, you will not marry an unsaved person. But there are many other reasons. God told the Israelites not to marry people from the unbelieving nations around them (see Deut. 7:3). Remember all the problems that plagued them for disobeying?

Not a week goes by that I do not receive letters and phone calls from Christians who, like the Israelites of old, are suffering the miserable consequences of being "unequally yoked together" with an unbeliever. You don't have to make that mistake!

A truly happy life-relationship becomes enhanced greatly when a boy friend or girl friend is not simply saved but is also actively living a consistent Christian life. Just how spiritual is the one you intend to marry?

1. Does he or she read the Bible and pray daily?
2. What about regular church attendance?
3. Does he or she share personal testimony with others?
4. What about obedience to the Word of God in general?

A strong Christian mate will be able to give valuable spiritual leadership to the family. When problems come up in your marriage, a godly mate will be able to discern the basic spiritual direction involved, then deal with them effectively. This ability is especially important, even if you are spiritually strong yourself.

What about the importance of a spiritual mate when God blesses your home with children? Proverbs 22:6 promises that *if* a child is trained up in the way he should go, he will not depart from it when he is old. Only spiritual parents can give that kind of training. All too often children who are not reared according to biblical principles grow up to bring anguish and shame .to both themselves and their parents. If you're not sure the one you now love will be that kind of a parent, you had better not marry him or her.

Using the chart below, you may rate your potential partner from one to ten (one being the lowest and ten the highest) on each item.

I hope this checklist helps you in considering a person's suitability as a marriage partner. You would do well to think seriously about your friend's personality characteristics. When dating, you can give continual attention to each of these areas. When you are with the person, consider as much evidence as possible to substantiate each of the ten items. If you enter marriage with plans to change your mate, you will probably be disappointed, because most personality characteristics don't change easily after adulthood unless a person has a serious encounter with Jesus Christ or seeks professional help.

Some people may think that evaluating a potential mate in this way is too objective an approach to such an emotional subject. But that is part of my point here. Marriage is a serious step and requires serious consideration. Marriage should be forever, and the spouses should have a joyful, fulfilled life together.

Admittedly, life—and marriage—may not *always* be a bed of roses, but there is absolutely no need for a marriage to become a field of battle. If Christian partners know a lot about each other before their marriage and if their marriage rests firmly on biblical precepts, they will be better able to deal with problems as they arise. They will be able to gain from their mutual gifts and become a blessing to each other and to their children. They will be able to say with Alfred, Lord Tennyson that "marriages are made in Heaven."

By studying this list and looking seriously for evidence, you may be able to avoid a lifetime of heartaches and problems.

A PREMARRIAGE CHECKLIST

	Poor			Average				Good		
Adjustment	1	2	3	4	5	6	7	8	9	10
Goals in Life	1	2	3	4	5	6	7	8	9	10
Intelligence	1	2	3	4	5	6	7	8	9	10
Education	1	2	3	4	5	6	7	8	9	10
Vocation	1	2	3	4	5	6	7	8	9	10
Health	1	2	3	4	5	6	7	8	9	10
Talents	1	2	3	4	5	6	7	8	9	10
Family	1	2	3	4	5	6	7	8	9	10
Friends	1	2	3	4	5	6	7	8	9	10
Spirituality	1	2	3	4	5	6	7	8	9	10

CHAPTER
5

Overcoming Mate Hate

Someone has said that the worst thing about marriage is that it involves two people!

And, of course, there is some truth in that statement. Marriage can bring some of the greatest joys in the world— loving another person, caring for another person, helping another person, and, in many ways, ministering to that person. Marriage may also be enhanced by sons and daughters. What a privilege to care for a tiny infant or to help a toddler to walk and talk or to explain things to an inquisitive child or to be a good friend to a teen-age son or daughter or to see young people grow up to be servants of God.

But marriage can also be painful; filled with problems. As I pointed out in the discussion of the premarriage checklist, evaluating a potential spouse in certain key areas is a good idea. In that way one is less likely to marry the wrong person, and many serious problems will be averted. Yet in virtually all marriages, problems of some kind will arise.

The ways in which people deal with their problems vary widely. Some couples may be able to acknowledge and solve even severe problems with little or no help from a professional. Others may choose to ignore a problem until it has grown to such proportions that it can no longer be ignored. It may require twice as long for a solution to take effect as it should have. The delay only complicated the initial problem and probably caused other problems in the meantime. Too many couples seem to "cope" with their problems by falling into patterns of what I call "mate hate." Their marriage is strained to the utmost, and unhappiness and dissatisfaction with self and spouse characterize their feelings. Let's look at some of the major problems that can create these feelings within a marriage and some of the possible solutions to resolve them.

Sexual Problems

One of the biggest stumbling blocks to marital happiness is sexual incompatibility and sexual unfulfillment. It is widely believed that most marital problems can be traced to the bedroom and to the extent a spouse is sexually fulfilled. Most people think that an answer to the question "How's your sex life?" is the one that really gets to the root of the problem, but this is rarely true.

In fact, most marital conflicts do not stem from a couple's sex life. Most sex problems are not really sex problems. Sex is just one part of life; it does not exist independently. Most sex problems in marriage are reflections of deeper personality maladjustments.

If one hundred people were gathered in a room, I wouldn't have to ask each one individually about his or her sex life to know who was sexually fulfilled. Instead, by giving personality and psychological tests, I could probably tell which people were struggling in their sex lives and, more importantly, get closer to the reasons why. People with personality hang-ups and deficiencies are most likely to have problems with sex in their marriages. Men and women who love the Lord and who are emotionally well adjusted are likely to have few sex problems.

Helen is a very nervous person. She constantly frets about something. When in a group, she worries about her appearance, what she should say, and her husband's or children's behavior. At home she is beset by the condition of the house, the neighbor complaining about the dog's barking, and the children not eating their breakfast. Worry, worry, worry. Nearly every part of life carries with it some anxiety.

It's no surprise to find that Helen is unhappy with her sex life. The bundle of nerves she carries all day, she takes into the bedroom at night. She cannot relax. She worries about making her husband happy. She recalls the times she couldn't adequately perform and fears the same thing may happen again. She can't get the kids, the neighbors, and other thoughts out of her head so she feels guilty about her lack of concentration and appreciation for the moment. Her husband is frustrated because she's tense and unresponsive; he goes to sleep upset and wakes up grumpy. He leaves for the office without saying good-bye, and Helen worries about their strained morning as she starts another anxious day.

The sex problem in Helen's marriage is actually caused by her constant state of anxiety. What causes her nervousness is another question, but as you can see, we are closer to dealing with the true problem by focusing on the anxiety rather than on sex. She will not find a real, lasting solution to her sexual difficulties until her personality problems are resolved.

Bob is chronically depressed. His is not just a case of "Monday morning blues"; Bob has a negative and "down" attitude six days out of seven. Rather than being cheerful and enjoying life, Bob is overly sensitive to bad news and derogatory comments. Things don't have to be going bad in order for Bob to be despondent. He's pessimistic and often discourages himself with his own thoughts. He only sees the rough roads and bad turns, seldom the good things.

Bob has an unhappy sex life too. People who are happy and content with life most of the time are able to function better sexually than those who are depressed and moody. Bob enters into lovemaking with little enthusiasm and few expectations. He has little interest in making his wife happy and feels he is incapable of satisfying her.

Bob's lack of sexual fulfillment is basically a reflection or symptom of a greater problem: depression. If Bob could enter the bedroom at night having felt positive and satisfied about the day, his approach to sex would be more optimistic and the results more fulfilling.

Consider a person who is inhibited, shy, or reclusive. This individual is more apt to experience sexual problems than one who is outgoing and friendly. The introvert who is uneasy about sharing her thoughts with her husband is also inhibited about sharing herself sexually. She feels overwhelmed by the intimacy of the situation. She feels vulnerable. Naturally she finds the romantic experience threatening. The withdrawn, shy person may feel that her partner is superior or demanding. Consequently, the person's inhibited personality, not sex, is the problem.

Barbara has a strained sexual relationship with her husband. Her problem is her inflexibility. It's not always noticeable in public because she usually ventures only into areas where she feels comfortable and secure. If she were given certain tests, they would show that she is resistant to change. She has trouble relating to new ideas and situations. She's unable to relax and adjust. It is as though she has her life in neat little squares and is threatened anytime she has to do things differently from her usual way. Changes in plans unsettle her. These feelings are carried over into her sex life. Barbara's sex problems can be traced to her inflexible personality.

John has no doubts about his marriage, but his wife does. Most psychologists would describe John as hostile. He speaks his mind, no matter whom he offends. He's usually negative. He often gets angry at his kids or his coworkers. Some men who are basically hostile keep it inside, but John lets it all come out. A hard worker? Yes. Good to his neighbors? Yes, but rough, outspoken, and negative.

His hostility reveals itself in many ways, including sexual ways. If John didn't have this personality problem, he would be a better lover. As it is, nothing seems to turn out right, including times of intimacy. He turns his wife off, which upsets him further. John's sex problems really aren't sex problems; they are hostility problems.

Another personality (and health) condition which reveals itself sexually is lethargy. Joan has this problem. Instead of being vibrant and energetic, she's unusually apathetic and slow moving. She is a nice person, but rather dull and uninteresting. She loves her husband Harry as much as she is capable of loving, but since she finds life languid, nothing excites her, not even sex.

Consider a person with low self-esteem. He is overwhelmed by the world. He looks at himself with doubts and skepticism. He believes he is incapable of living up to anyone's expectations. You can imagine his feelings regarding sex. He already feels inadequate. Any negative comments his wife makes only add to his feelings of inferiority. He wonders if he understands his wife, physically and emotionally. His self-doubts mount until he is affected physically and is unable to perform. Eventually, sex in the marriage almost disappears.

Couples may be able to adapt their social and family lives and to some extent work around the wife's anxiety or the husband's hostility. But they can't adjust or hide in the bedroom. Why should people with unfulfilled sex lives seek professional help? For the same reason a person with chest pains should see a doctor. A problem exists that needs to be solved so that the individuals can have more fulfilled lives.

Most psychologists and psychiatrists don't need to delve into a patient's sex life, because that is not necessarily where the problem lies. A psychiatrist friend has told me: "I've worked with lots of people on their sex problems, but the word *sex* rarely comes up. By helping people resolve their personality problems, their sex life improves remarkably."

Some couples have medical problems that require attention, and some benefit significantly from technical counsel. Others need a devoted life in Christ so that they are at peace with themselves and God. Couples who are in patterns of mate hate should look at all areas of their lives and give special attention to personality maladjustments which all too often are reflected in problems with sex.

Bones of Contention

Not all family problems are deep psychological problems or personality maladjustments. Opposite views in many areas can lead to recurring quarrels and growing bitterness in a marriage. Let's consider a few of these differences and the problems they can cause.

Punctuality

I once knew a young man who couldn't be on time for his own funeral. He was always late. He was tardy for school, baseball practice, band rehearsal—you name it—he never could be on time. To top it off, this habit never bothered him. If the concert began without him as second trumpet or the ball game began without him at second base, he understood and never made a fuss.

When he married, he chose a girl who was the exact opposite in regard to punctuality. You could set your clock by her, and she *hated* being late. If she knew she was going to walk into an event after it had started, she often chose not to show up at all.

This couple eventually got a divorce. Of course, this issue of punctuality was not the sole reason for their separation, but I do know it caused many arguments and plenty of hurt feelings. Neither of them seemed willing to change. She couldn't plan a schedule because he wasn't reliable. Many times they missed going to parties or other outings because she wouldn't show up late and he couldn't arrive on time.

Special Occasions

A good deal of reconciling may be involved in the celebration of holidays, birthdays, and other special occasions. One spouse may like to remember special dates with big parties and lots of fanfare. The other may feel a card, flowers, or a quiet evening at home is more appropriate if, in fact, he or she remembers the occasion at all!

Joan's family always opened their presents on Christmas Eve. Don's parents made the children wait until after the big Christmas Day dinner. Which spouse is going to break tradition so that the new family can celebrate the holidays in happiness?

Tidiness

Some habits may have to be changed in order to avoid arguments. Tidiness is one example. Peter's mother kept an immaculate house. "A place for everything, and everything in its place" was her motto. Margaret, on the other hand, grew up in a very informal setting. As long as the pathways leading from room to room remained clear, things were fine at her mother's house.

Peter and Margaret will argue over not only the neatness of their home but also who will do the cleaning. Margaret won't be bothered by the mess, so she will not clean it up. Peter will eventually get tired of picking up after his wife and confront her. Can you hear the argument?

OVERCOMING MATE HATE

Personal Appearance

The husband likes dressing down, while the wife enjoys dressing up. He only wears shoes when required and never touches ties. He prefers T-shirts and shorts, but he will put on jeans if it's cold. She doesn't mind being comfortable, but she wants to look her best, especially when she's out in public.

However, she won't go out with him dressed so informally, and he won't go anywhere that requires dress attire. They stay at home, angry with each other instead of going out and enjoying themselves with friends.

Values and Goals

Some problems result directly from one partner's values and goals, which dictate the direction the family will go.

Ed has a good job with a warehouse. He started working there when he dropped out of high school, and he has worked his way up to truck driver. He is in line for the shipping supervisor position when the present boss retires. He is a good provider for his young family, and he is satisfied with his accomplishments.

His wife, Sharon, only graduated from high school, but she has higher aspirations. She wants to go to college someday and start a career. She also has plans for her two children to earn college degrees and pursue professional careers, so she emphasizes school work and makes sure they study hard.

"I don't see why you have to push them so hard," Ed complains. "They're only kids. They should be enjoying their childhood more. I hate to see them spend so much time with their noses stuck in books. I'm doing okay, and I don't need school. Besides that, I probably take home more dough than most of those eggheads teaching up at that college."

You can see the type of problems Ed's attitude toward education is going to cause. Now it affects the raising of the children. What will happen later when his wife decides to leave the house and walk down the academic road with a degree?

Discipline of Children

Differing views on discipline may lead to difficulties in raising children. "My father always spanked us kids when we needed it," Carol remembers. "It taught us to mind and respect our parents."

Eric doesn't agree. "Spanking only made me more angry and rebellious. They beat me to a pulp, and I'm not going to do that to my kids."

Such opposite opinions cause nagging problems in what otherwise could be a happy marriage. If Carol is the only parent who spanks, the children may grow up to resent her, or the children will receive different signals from their parents, and they may become disciplinary problems because they are never sure what to expect from bad behavior.

These are just a few examples of differences that couples may bring into marriage. Two fine people literally can bring a whole world of differences into their union if the two come from different worlds. These differences need to be reconciled and the problems resolved if a couple is to avoid mate hate.

Home Life

Some men function much worse after a child is born into the family. His latent jealousy comes to the surface, and he blames his wife and often strikes her to "get her attention." Sometimes his rage extends to the child. In some instances, the husband's jealousy of the child is not without foundation. Experienced counselors have heard many husbands say, "I had a marriage up until the time our first child was born. But after that it was all different. My wife spent most of her time with our daughter and looked to her for affection. I began to feel like a third wheel on a two-wheel bicycle. Nearly all of my wife's attention has turned on our daughter." It's true that some parents have more interest in their child than they do in their mate. This is not to excuse the husband's violent behavior, but it does provide an explanation for it.

Other problems in a marriage develop when a child has special problems that have not been properly diagnosed. After years of quarreling and fighting about a child, many parents are ready to call it quits and get a divorce. Instead of seeking professional help for themselves or for their child, they continue to argue and disagree until they reach divorce court. How much better it is in such families to seek professional help and determine what can be done for the child, or how the parents can be helped.

This problem is usually compounded when the mother is working outside the home. Yet today in the United States two-thirds of all women between twenty-five and forty-four are employed outside the home. As a result, the wife may be carrying a double load. In addition to her work throughout the day, she may find herself having to work late into the evening at home while she is tired and unhappy. This situation can spill over into many facets of family living concerning the children as well as the spouse.

Spiritual Diversity

Through the years I have counseled husbands and wives who have been unequally yoked spiritually. Perhaps she has grown in the Lord and desires to have a closer relationship with Christ and to lead her family into godly paths. But the unsaved husband has different motivations, and he sees his wife's new behavior through unsaved glasses. For example, an unsaved man said to me recently, "Heck, since my wife's gotten religion we don't have any more fun. 'No liquor,' she says. And she has a great big list of things she and I are not supposed to do and the kids are not supposed to do. I don't feel comfortable about bringing friends in any more because she gets so upset when we have a little drink. And there's hardly anything we can attend together any more except baseball games. She doesn't seem to mind those. And furthermore, she tries to drag the kids to her way of thinking. Then on Sunday morning she's pulling them out of bed and taking them to Sunday school. I don't know if she'll ever get over this or not, but it sure throws a wet blanket on most of the things I want to do."

This problem is serious because the marriage partner who has come to know and love Christ can never go back into a world of sinful pleasures, and the unsaved husband cannot understand how nearly everything he does is wrong. Solutions to these problems require a great deal of thoughtful action and prayer on the part of the spouse who is saved. He or she can usually benefit from the wise counsel of a pastor or another person who can help him or her to maintain his or her testimony for Christ and at the same time be as loving as possible with the mate.

Solving Marriage Problems

For awhile, Paula tried to tell herself that her marriage was okay. She and Bill weren't really getting along as well as she would like, but she rationalized that all married couples went through rough times. But those times stretched into months, and things were definitely not getting better. There was no denying it: their marriage was disintegrating. She tried to discuss it with Bill, but he just shrugged it off.

Then one day while listening to a radio talk show, Paula heard a marriage counselor say, "Even if your spouse isn't interested in changing, that's no reason why you shouldn't improve yourself. Look at your own life. See what part you play in the problems, and do what you can to change yourself."

That started Paula thinking. She began to consider how she reacted to Bill's actions. She also thought about how some of her remarks affected him.

She sent for a cassette by the counselor and gained more insight into herself and her marriage. At a local Christian bookstore she purchased a book which helped her. In short, she began changing her attitude and behavior.

Several months passed, and Paula began noticing little changes in Bill. Their arguments were less frequent. She had made an effort to hold back criticism, and in unknowing response, Bill wasn't losing his temper as often. He still refused to believe that the marriage had serious problems, but his attitude had changed enough that he agreed to accompany Paula to a weekend seminar on marriage and the family.

This example of Bill and Paula not only can give hope to those who feel discouraged about their marriage, but it also illustrates some steps that can be taken to solve marriage problems.

1. *Admit problems exist.* For a long time, Paula refused to believe her marriage had problems that required special help. She knew that no marriage was perfect, but finally she accepted the fact her marriage wasn't even healthy. The first step in solving a problem is to recognize that there *is* a problem. If things aren't the way they should be with your spouse, ask yourself why. Don't be ashamed to face up to the fact that problems exist.

2. *Examine yourself.* Though Bill was unresponsive, Paula began to look for ways she could make the marriage better. Often a spouse will be quick to say, "My husband (or wife) needs help," yet fails to see personal weaknesses. A marriage involves two people, and it will take two people to eventually resolve all the difficulties. In my years of counseling I have noticed that it is usually the wife who takes the first step to seek help. Interestingly, I have rarely seen a husband *not* follow her in getting help when he finally decides there is a problem. It only stands to reason that the spouse who has the insight is the one who must make the first move.

3. *Take advantage of available resources.* God has gifted many people with the ability to counsel troubled couples, and these counselors have produced many helpful materials and programs that can help smooth rough marriages. Christian bookstores carry outstanding books and cassettes designed to improved troubled marriages. Some authors have their own radio or television broadcasts. Some are now entering into the up-and-coming video-tape ministry.

Other counselors have had success in conducting seminars. Many churches sponsor local weekend sessions open to the public. Even better than a weekend seminar is a week-long, uninterrupted conference like that available at the Narramore Christian Foundation. Our conference for business and professional people is held three times a year and offers counseling and instruction in an ideal environment. Couples as well as singles come from across the United States to live on our campus for a week. Away from the pressures of work and family and among the often-needed change of scenery, they take psychological tests and take inventory of their own adjustments. They have private and group counseling and attend sessions offered by a large staff of psychologists, physicians, and other specialists.

4. *Get individual counseling.* Some long-standing problems

deserve individual attention through professional counseling. Meeting one-on-one with a licensed professional whose practice is based on God's Word can produce excellent returns.

Life is short. There is little reason why a person cannot receive professional help. Various types are available, but the biggest deterrent in seeking help is the desire to get it.

I am not only encouraged but also excited about the couples salvaging their marriages. I have seen so many husbands and wives, who were on the brink of divorce, get help and in time develop happy, God-blessed marriages.

Less than a year ago, I was holding an all-day Saturday seminar in a city in Florida. Unknown to me at that time, a woman who was within a month or so of getting a divorce came into the auditorium. A few minutes later she looked across the room, and much to her surprise, she saw her husband. Both were Christians. *Will wonders never cease*, she thought. They had hardly spoken to each other in months.

A moment later she looked around, and she saw her oldest daughter and her husband. Absolutely surprised, she wondered how they had heard about the seminar.

Well, if that weren't enough, she next saw her son and his wife. She was sure that none of them knew the others were there.

About that time I went to the platform, greeted everyone, and started the seminar. At midmorning I asked each person to take a self-scoring personality inventory test. When everyone had done this, I showed them how to score their own tests. "Now," I said, "I would like all husbands and wives to scatter throughout the auditorium and privately discuss your test scores. Please don't sit near any other couple." I knew this would bring a lot of insight because I had asked each to mark not only themselves but also their spouse.

The woman who was about to get the divorce looked across the sanctuary at her husband and then walked over to him. He agreed to discuss the test with her. For the first time in their thirty-five-year marriage, he discovered how she felt about herself in about twenty-five areas. He also learned how she felt about him. There were some real surprises!

The same thing happened as he shared his scores about himself and his feelings about her. She was surprised at several things he said about himself—and about her. They began to discover some misconceptions and erroneous attitudes they had been holding.

The next morning I was in my hotel room, getting ready to go to a local church to speak, when the phone rang. It was the husband. He told me what had happened the day before, and he wanted to make reservations at another of my conferences for the next week. He concluded by asking, "Do you have anything special to help us?"

Then I shared the fact that we always had three licensed Christian psychologists at the Bible conference to conduct private counseling. I also explained that other professionals would be giving group psychological tests and conducting small group therapy for anyone who wanted it.

"Put us down for everything you've got," he said. "We both gained a lot of insight yesterday at the seminar and we want to continue it."

Their experiences the next week at the conference were concentrated. Psychological tests provided an accurate diagnosis of their real problems. They had private counseling sessions (usually separately) each day as well as group counseling. This was in addition to Bible messages each morning, gospel music, plus afternoon and evening sessions on everyday problems.

The first day, Monday, they walked around the campus talking. By Wednesday they were holding hands, and by Friday they were almost inseparable! By the end of the week they both gave testimonies about the insights they had gained and the changes they were beginning to see in their lives. They began living together again, and about four months later they showed up at our Rosemead, California, campus to take a week of training for business people. Today they are happy and serving the Lord!

This is what can happen and *does* happen when people get professional help. I've seen it happen hundreds of times. Problems have deep-rooted causes, and they deserve individual, professional counseling. Indeed, every couple having severe problems should get professional help as this couple did. Just as the Lord uses godly men to preach the gospel, so He uses godly psychologists and others to help resolve marriage problems. Mate hate can resolve and turn into spousal arousal!

CHAPTER

6

The Young and Impressionable

In the summer of 1982, my wife Ruth and I took a tour group to mainland China. For her it was like a homecoming, since she had been raised there during the early years of her childhood and her first language was Chinese. One thing about our visit that will always stand out in our minds was the respect and love the Chinese people showed to their children.

In that country couples are discouraged, in fact almost prohibited, from having more than one child. So children are really precious to them. Everywhere we traveled, fathers and mothers would lift their little tot above their heads so they could see the Americans and so we could see their baby. Although they live in a communist country where the Bible is virtually eliminated, these little ones are getting a loving start in life.

We often hear the statement that our children are our future, and indeed they are. God tells us how very important children are when He says, "Behold, children are a heritage from the LORD/The fruit of the womb is His reward" (Ps. 127:3). In other words, God gives us children; we inherit them from Him; they are His very special possession; and we as adults are to train them and guide them as a special heritage from the Lord Himself. Yet many children get a poor start in life because they are mistreated and abused.

Police officials, Christian leaders, and even politicians are warning the nation about the rising incidence of child abuse. Every day in the offices of psychologists, psychiatrists, social workers, pastors, and other counselors, people are telling about the cruelties they suffered at the hands of their family members. Just when a counselor thinks he's heard nearly everything, he is told about another way someone has been mistreated. Many researchers say that the incidence of family trouble will probably intensify.

Recently I received a letter that tells us volumes about child abuse. Every sentence is significant, but the last one is especially noteworthy.

> As a little girl, I was made to get into a big box after a severe beating from my father. I heard him putting things on the top so I couldn't get out.
>
> It seemed like an eternity that I was in there. I felt sick inside the stuffy box without any air.
>
> When my dad came and finally opened the box, he wanted to know if I wanted out.
>
> Of course I said "yes." Then he gave me another beating. My dad always carried a strap in his pocket. And believe you me, we got it.
>
> I didn't find out until I was grown, what it was all about. Finally I learned that if my mother wouldn't let him have sex about every night, he would take it out on us kids the next day.
>
> I had those belt eyelet prints, black and blue, showing upon my legs every now and then all through childhood. So you see, I don't have very good memories of my dad. I guess, too, it's no wonder I have so much trouble with my legs.
>
> I am almost 75 years old now, but I can never forget those beatings which I didn't understand.

This woman's heart-wrenching statements detail her experiences of abuse as a young girl. The vividness with which she remembers them is evidence of just how long-lasting the effects of abuse can be. At seventy-five she still carries the deep scars within herself, even though the bruises on her legs have long since disappeared.

Each time we hear about new instances of child abuse we can hardly believe our ears. Rather than loving and nurturing a child and making him feel warm and wanted, some parents are abusing their child and most likely injuring him for a lifetime.

What can you as a Christian do to prevent it? You must learn to recognize some of the signs of abuse. I will discuss some ways to do this so that you may have a general guide to go by. Child abuse is not just physical. You may indeed help a child because you may be the only person to notice the abuse has been or is taking place. Report any cases to your local police or a social welfare agency.

Why do parents and other caregivers abuse children entrusted to them? The reasons are many and complex, and we will look at some of them in an attempt to understand them. Any problem must be fully examined before a viable solution can be proposed. The problem of child abuse is no exception.

Physical Abuse

Angela's parents had been arguing all evening, and the shy little girl had been unable to sleep. Through the thin partition separating her bedroom from the living room, the six-year-old girl heard her father screaming obscenities, and she pulled the covers tightly over her head.

As his yelling grew louder, Angela heard her father strike her mother, who reacted with long, choking sobs. Angela felt enraged that her father would hit her mother, and she couldn't believe that anyone would want to hurt her. So she crawled out of bed.

"Leave Mommy alone," Angela screamed, standing beside her bedroom door. "I don't love you, Daddy, when you hurt Mommy!"

"Get back to bed, Angela, before I beat you too," her father warned.

Angela screamed at her father again, and she tried to run into her bedroom. But her father caught her by the arm and threw her across the room.

Being thrown around a room is only one of many ways that children can be abused. I have put together a descriptive list of some of the other ways, but the list is by no means complete. It is sufficient, I think, to show how approximately one million children suffer each year. And this list should give you something to look for in case you ever suspect that a child you know, either at church or in the neighborhood, is being abused.

Breaking or Fracturing Bones

Long bones of an arm or leg can be twisted, resulting in a spiral fracture. A child's bones can also be chipped from abuse. Back rib fractures are common when young children have been physically mistreated. Sometimes these breaks and fractures go unnoticed until a physician takes an X-ray.

Burning and Scalding

Because children instinctively withdraw from pain, burns that cover a large portion of the body should be questioned. When children are scalded, they are often held against their will, and either boiling water is poured over them or they are forceably immersed into a bathtub filled with hot water. These kinds of burns may leave "sock" or "glove" marks on the child's body. Some people burn children with cigarettes or hot irons on the stomach, arms, legs, and feet.

Striking with Objects

If children are struck with a heavy object, they may incur deep muscular bruises or they may hemorrhage. Usually these kinds of injuries are hard to gauge because there may be no sign of abuse except that the child complains of pain. Medical experts say that evidence of such abuse is detectable in only about one-half of the cases, and it's often best to play it safe and have a child examined for serious internal injuries to his kidneys, liver, and other vital organs.

All too frequently, a child is discovered with rope burns around his neck because guardians have attempted to hang him, or a child has been punished by being whipped with an electrical cord, bicycle chain, or belt buckle. Loop marks on a child's body are caused if an electrical cord or belt has been doubled over and applied, while wraparound marks signify that a whiplike object has been used.

Striking a child with any of these objects is likely to cause bruises, and frequently a child may have multiple bruises.

Multiple bruises can be of the same color or of different colors, reflecting when the child was abused and the various stages of their healing.

- For the first few hours after a child has been struck, the bruise will appear *red*.
- Within six to twelve hours after an injury, the bruise will appear *blue*.
- After twelve to twenty-four hours, the injury will turn a *black-purple* color.
- Usually after four to six days, the bruise will turn a *dark green* tint.
- And after five to ten days, the bruise will turn a *pale green* or *yellow*.

Bruises usually have a pattern and may take on the outline

of a hairbrush or hand, or the long, thin pattern of an object used as a whip.

Bashing

Many children are simply bashed against a wall or a floor, leaving them unconscious with a concussion or a cracked skull.

Shaking and Whiplashing

You've probably seen a parent grab his child by the shoulders and shake him severely. This kind of abuse is very subtle and may be difficult to detect. Physicians say prolonged shaking may cause intracranial and intraocular hemorrhaging or even deafness, blindness, paralysis, or death. If the child survives, by the time he goes to school he may have learning disabilities due to neurological injuries.

Puncturing

Abused children may be stuck with pins or stabbed with a sharp implement, resulting in the child's need to be rushed to a hospital.

You may use the following list as a further guide if you suspect that a child is being battered. Any one of the items is a warning signal that should be heeded.

- Are there bruises that can't be explained?
- Does the child wear long sleeves to cover up scars and injuries?
- Does he seem to want to tell you something, but can't do so?
- Does he complain of being sick?
- Is he not playing and being active?
- Does he mention having been to the doctor lately?
- Is he depressed?
- Does he appear unusually fearful?

- Is he not sleeping well?
- Does he have nightmares and frightening dreams?
- Does he cry a great deal?
- Does he avoid one or both parents?
- Recently, does he wet the bed or urinate frequently?
- Does he stutter or give evidence of other speech problems that were not present before?
- Has he recently lost his appetite?
- Does he complain of headaches?
- Does he limp or favor one arm?
- Does he complain of being sore or hurting?

Naturally, these symptoms can occasionally be seen to some extent in almost any healthy, happy child, but they are also signs that a child has been or is now being abused. These symptoms are especially significant if they are not a part of the child's usual way of acting, or if they continue to show themselves over a period of time.

After a child has been abused, his wounds heal over, often leaving telltale scars. Frequently, abused children will have scars on the backs of their arms and hands caused when they tried to defend themselves against attack. They often have scars on their backs, running from the neck to the knees.

Neglect

No matter how much we would like to deny it, we must acknowledge the fact that many people, including some parents, have little regard for children. This is verified by the fact that so many children are neglected. Even some respectable Christian families may neglect their children in subtle ways.

Some types of neglect are readily apparent, and social workers who deal with neglected children as opposed to outright abused children have checklists they consult when investigating general neglect cases. Here are some typical items on those lists:

1. Are meals prepared? Do children snack when hungry? Or is there any food at all in the home?
2. Are there unsanitary conditions in the home, such as garbage piled in the kitchen or animal and human excrement on the floor?
3. Is there plumbing or heating in the home? Is the house a fire hazard?
4. Do family members have a warm place to sleep?
5. Does the child need immediate medical and dental care?
6. Is the child always sleepy and hungry and seldom bathed?
7. Is the child's clothing dirty? Is it warm enough to protect him in cold weather?

Richard Parker, detective in charge of the child abuse unit, Los Angeles Police Department, remembers one of his first child neglect cases. After investigators learned that a seven-month-old child had starved to death in her family's home, Parker was asked to take the two-year-old sister into protective custody and later on to court.

"I speculate that the only reason she survived was because she was taller and snagged a piece of food now and then," Parker recalls. "And after I lifted her into the car and got her situated in the front seat, she scooted over to sit right next to me while we drove to court. And she kept pointing at her shoes. The pair we had given her was obviously the first pair she'd ever worn."

Social services statistics show that general neglect cases represent over 50 percent of their total workload. Surprisingly, child neglect is sometimes covered up in the interests of "not butting in" or "getting involved" with a family's personal business.

The likelihood that general neglect is the leading cause of childhood death in America is sometimes not readily apparent. When a child is brought to a hospital because of pneumonia or a high fever and then dies, the attending physician may never know that the child never had a warm place to sleep or clean clothes to wear. When the cause of death listed is a "respectable" disease, such as pneumonia, the contributing cause may never be accurately recorded.

Emotional Abuse

As a psychologist, I am especially interested in the emotional abuse of children. Thousands of letters come to my office telling of abuse the writer suffered as a child. Large numbers of pastors, missionaries, educators, business people, and others who have taken the two-week and one-week seminars at our Rosemead campus have told of their negative childhood experiences. And, of course, it shows in their attitudes and behavior.

Recently I had the privilege of serving on the Attorney General's Task Force on Family Violence. In this capacity I traveled with eight other leaders to major cities of the United States where we conducted hearings about problems in the family. We heard testimonies from victims, research specialists, and organizations serving the abused. Needless to say, this study, which lasted more than a year, was an unusual and enlightening experience. During each hearing my mind would turn to evangelical Christian churches and to Christian families throughout the United States.

"What about violence and abuse in the Christian home? Are born-again Christians sometimes abusive? If so, what is the most prevalent kind of abuse?"

Finally, I decided to send out a questionnaire to Christian families across America. Nearly twelve thousand people filled out the questionnaire and returned it to me. They not only answered the questionnaire but many of them wrote about the abuse they had experienced in their childhood.

I am convinced that although many Christian homes are not marked by violence, many of them do experience emotional abuse. In fact, many Christians may not realize that they are abusing their own sons and daughters. Following are twenty-two ways in which emotional abuse can be experienced by children—even in "good Christian" homes.

1. Yelling at a Child

How easy it is for parents to be verbally impatient with their child. Father shouts; mother screams, louder and louder, believing that the very force of their voices are going to mold the child into improvement. Of course, this isn't true, and most parents don't realize the emotional beating their child feels when all he hears is constant yelling.

2. Comparing a Child Unfavorably with Others

Your child may not be perfect, but telling him how good other children are isn't going to make him better. A child who makes a mistake only feels more inferior when he hears his mother telling him that his brother or sister or someone else never does such things. Not only will this tear down a child's self-image, but it will also hurt his relationship with his friends, whom he is told are better than he is. He is likely to carry these scars a lifetime.

3. Throwing Bible Verses at a Child

Some parents feel that constantly correcting their child with Bible verses is going to make him more conscious of his poor behavior. Actually the bombardment of verses may only make him feel frustrated and guilty, and he will develop a dislike for the Bible—a book that does nothing but tell him how bad he is. Scriptural "spankings" can cause a child to dislike church, Sunday school, and ultimately God. Children desperately need God's Word in their hearts and minds, but they shouldn't be getting it when the parent is feeling hostile and angry.

4. Ridiculing, Minimizing, and Criticizing a Child

Some parents may ridicule without even realizing it. Criticism comes easily. Although a certain amount of constructive criticism is helpful, a steady diet of negative words can only make a child feel inadequate, discouraged, and despondent. This is real emotional abuse.

5. Witholding Compliments

While it's easy to criticize, it's difficult for many parents to encourage. Parents who've never been complimented daily by their own fathers and mothers may find it strange, and even impossible to compliment their own children. Consequently, such children are abused passively. On the other hand, the complimented child will gain more confidence, feel more secure about himself, be more outgoing and eager to tackle challenges. Children who don't hear compliments, even if they don't hear criticism, lack motivation and a desire to achieve. This is often seen in substandard school work. A child may be intelligent enough but not have the interest or drive to do well in class or the playground.

6. Lying to a Child

Parents don't always realize what harm they are doing to a child when they lie to him. Children, especially young ones, believe that mommy or daddy can do almost anything. If everyone else in the world fails, dad and mom can always come through. How devastated that child is when he discovers that his parents have lied. Now whom can he trust? A child raised in an environment of untruthfulness has two strikes against him. He usually goes through life doubting others and himself. Such abuse is insidious and debilitating.

7. Continually Accusing and Blaming a Child

Parents who are unhappy or who have a shaky marriage may unconsciously use the children as scapegoats. If the kids can't be blamed, the parents at least can vent their frustrations on them. The children, of course, don't understand this. They just know that they are being blamed for things that they can't control. They usually grow up to feel guilty and insecure. These abused children tend to go through life as second-class citizens.

8. Using the Silent Treatment

A parent who is angry or disappointed in his son or daughter may decide not to speak to him for a while or until the child has done what he is told to do. Perhaps this silent treatment is better than flying off the handle, but since not talking usually includes not listening, the child is left bewildered, unable to find out what's wrong or defend himself. The silent treatment is degrading and abusive to a child because it puts him in the class with animals who cannot understand well or talk.

9. Repressing Emotions

"Don't cry." "Shut your mouth." "Keep still." "I don't want any crying." "I don't want to hear it." These are all abusive ways of keeping a child from expressing emotions. How frustrating it is for a child, who often doesn't know any other way of handling his feelings, not to be able to cry when he is hurt or shout when he's angry or sing when he is happy. By letting a child show his emotions, a parent learns how he feels. A child is healthiest when he can talk freely with his parent.

10. Questioning a Child's Salvation When He Misbehaves

"How can you say you love Jesus when you act like this? You say you're saved but you sure don't act like it. I doubt if you are." What a burden of guilt to place on a child. He may think he is no longer in God's family, or that his sins are too great for Jesus to forgive. A parent who threatens a child with such abusive and false statements is not only filling him with false ideas about his salvation but also misrepresenting God. Such an abused child begins to feel shaky and uncertain about his relationship with the Lord.

11. Not Listening to a Child

Teenagers often say to me, "My dad tells me what to do, but he never listens to anything I have to say." Perhaps parents are too busy to listen or simply not interested. The parent may think he has the important answers. More likely, the parent himself was never listened to when he was a child, so "listening" doesn't enter his mind. But children need to be heard. Not only does listening tell them they're worthwhile, it also tells them that what they have to say is important. This creates a communication line for the future and an ability, when they are grown and married, to talk and listen to their own son's and daughter's conversations.

12. Placing Undue Emphasis on Overachievement

Most parents don't realize that undue emphasis on overachievement is abuse. It is easy for parents to want or expect "the most of" their children. But what is "the most"? Often the goals we set for our children are our goals, not theirs. We praise overachievement but ignore simple accomplishment. There is nothing wrong with excellence. In fact, it is desirable; but parents must remember that a child is a child, and he takes three steps to their one. Rejection comes in many forms, and undue emphasis on overachievement is one.

13. Not Encouraging a Child to Talk

Perhaps as a child, you grew up in a home where children were seen and not heard—and not heard from. If so, you may not see the value or feel comfortable having conversations with your child. However, not talking to your child will keep you at a distance. What better way is there to find out what your child thinks, believes, and feels than talking with him? When a child talks, he relieves himself of his strong feelings. He also thinks as he talks. He refines his ideas, and he comes to think of himself in a healthier, happier way. Failure to encourage talking is a form of abuse.

14. Continually Threatening a Child

Some parents feel the best way to handle their child is to threaten him with physical punishment—whether it be a spanking or grounding or no dessert. These parents don't realize the problems that their tongue abuse may be creating for their parent-child relationship. First, they may be developing a feeling of dislike in the child—a dislike for the parent. How would you feel about someone who was constantly threatening to take all the good things away from you or threatening you with pain? Secondly, the parent may be creating a constant feeling of fear in the child; or, if the parent doesn't carry out those threats, an attitude of "nothing will happen to me." Both can cause greater problems as the child grows older.

15. Showing Favoritism to One Child

There are obvious cases of favoritism, like Jacob and Esau in the Bible. And the problems this can create are clear. (Poor relations with his brothers was Joseph's.) But sometimes parents can show favoritism without knowing it. For example, praising one child for his *A* in school and ignoring the other's *B*. Or a child may see the favoritism and not understand why it exists. Children, like adults, don't like it when things are unfair. Yet many parents show partiality to a particular child because the youngster responds better to the parent. Sometimes a child unconsciously reminds the parent of someone whom the parent dislikes. And, of course, favoritism pits one child against another and prevents brothers' and sisters' having close relationships—even in adulthood.

16. Calling a Child Names

Fewer things can do more damage to a child's self-esteem than name calling. A child who constantly hears Mother calling him "stupid," "lazy," "peewee," or "clumsy" will eventually believe her and lose confidence, or he'll start to resent her and begin using the same words on her. I know a woman who, as a child, was always called "idiot." Her older sister called her that, and later her father and mother. Eventually the whole family called her the name. I know another whose mother always introduced her (as a child) as "the unwanted one." Such abuse lasts many years.

17. Failing to Keep Promises

Just as lying can destroy a child's trust in his parents, so can the parent's failure to keep a promise. Parents may make promises without thinking, or they may forget what they've promised. But a child seldom forgets such things. A parent that continually breaks promises will soon find his child hard to control and uncooperative. Why should a son be faithful to his father when his father isn't faithful in return?

18. Allowing No Court of Appeal

"I don't want to hear any more about it. The matter is settled; I've made up my mind and that's that." There are times when a final no is important and necessary. But some parents feel it is necessary to slam the door on any debate that may question their authority. Obviously, children shouldn't run the home, but allowing no "court of appeal" may lead to continued resentment and hostility.

19. Threatening a Child Through Guilt or "Love"

Have you heard these: "After all I've done for you, now you do this"; "God doesn't love you because you're like that"; "If you want mother (or Jesus) to love you...."

By making a child feel guilty, parents sometimes can make the child do certain things. But if he hears such things often enough, what effect will it have on him? He may become callous and indifferent, seeing how such feelings are so easily tossed around. Or he may be so afraid of hurting others' feelings that he won't get involved. What an abusive burden—going through life feeling you can't measure up, feeling you're guilty and to blame.

20. Demanding Perfection

Many parents are perfectionists. They may have grown up with perfectionist mothers. Or they may not feel really good about themselves, so they continually do little things to make themselves feel better. But whatever the cause, it is harmful to the child. A youngster who lives with a perfectionist parent usually feels rejected—many times a day. Constantly scolding a child for his shortcomings shows him his faults, but it offers no solution.

21. Manipulating a Child

Some parents "use" their child to accomplish their own desires. They set the stage so that the child will do what the parents want him to do. This is rather simple when the child is young, but as he gets older, the parents may find the child overly dependent or resentful. Such abuse is damaging to a child because it minimizes him.

A child who is continually manipulated comes to dislike the parent who does it. And so often, he or she becomes a manipulator.

22. Questioning and Ridiculing a Child's Commitment to Christ

The Bible tells us that God called Samuel at an early age. David, too, was still a youth when he killed Goliath. Even Jesus was about His Father's business at an early age. Youngsters can have a sincere desire to serve God. But some parents may ridicule or challenge their child's faith. The toughest opposition to our faith can come from our families.

One of the most serious mistakes a parent can make is to question a child's commitment to Christ, if indeed he is saved or seeking to serve the Lord. Many men and women have been "turned off" in their Christian walk because as children they were discouraged unduly by unhappy or unthinking parents.

In summary, these are some of the common ways parents abuse their children emotionally. The bruises may not be so apparent as in beatings. But the invisible scars left on their personalities are usually more ugly and long lasting. Childhood emotional abuse can affect a person as long as he lives.

Why Adults Abuse Children

Experts know that there is no simple explanation of why adults abuse children. However, after much study of the problem, they have been able to identify several basic reasons, and I will mention some of them here.

Learned Behavior

Research shows that people who abuse children have usually seen abuse themselves as children. Growing up, they often saw their parents quarreling, fighting, and abusing each other. Not only that, but the child himself was abused. He was slapped, beaten, or hurt in various ways.

The child has now become a husband and father, and he's acting much as his parents did years before. In a sense, they have taught him how to act. They gave him hands-on lessons in how to respond in tight, angry spots at home, and now he doesn't see anything wrong with carrying on the way he does. It's natural to him.

He may have come to believe, for example, that when his mother "got it" from his dad, she probably deserved it. Because his mother nagged at him and made life miserable for him, he may have come to believe that although she was abused, she had actually asked for it. Who knows the rationalization that takes place in the minds of family members where there are many relationships, dynamics, problems, and injustices?

Low Self-esteem

When you notice a person acting in a certain way, either in a desirable or an undesirable manner, you can be quite sure that his behavior is a reflection of how he feels about himself down deep. His low self-esteem or his high self-esteem dictate to a great extent his thinking, feeling, and acting. It is rare indeed to find parents who beat their children if those same parents have high self-concepts and healthy, happy feelings toward themselves.

An adult who feels he's no good, always wrong, disliked, stupid, and unloved is likely to become an abuser. It's easy for such a person to lash out at the kids, knock them down, throw things at them, and mistreat them in a dozen ways. This also gives us a clue to the kind of counseling needed. Therapy with a perpetrator should usually center in his feelings about himself—his self-esteem.

Hostile and Negative Feelings

For many years, the Narramore Christian Foundation has

maintained a large counseling center. During this time, people from around the nation have come for private counseling. In a great percentage of these cases psychological tests showed that clients had hostile and negative feelings, but most of them were unaware of their hostile attitudes.

Negative feelings in a person do not come and go. They actually developed hour by hour, day by day, month by month, and year by year as the person was growing up. By the time he became an adult, the negative, caustic feelings were imbedded deeply inside. Finally they became persistent.

Parents who are hostile don't have to think about being angry. These personality traits have become built in, and they show up in every area of life. Remarkably, they even show up in the lives of people who have been born again, who are attending church, and who are trying to live the Christian life. I might add that such people are not angry and hostile because they are Christians. *If they weren't Christians, their hostility would be much worse.*

Unhappy Marriages

When I was growing up, I remember hearing my mother say, "There are more people who are married than are doing well." Perhaps I didn't understand her statement too well as a child. But now, years later, as a psychologist who has counseled many people, I believe I understand what she meant.

Many people have unwisely or unknowingly married the wrong person, or they have married too early. Some have failed to get professional help to make their marriage better. In many instances they have not sought the Lord fully.

Such unhappy married people may fly off the handle and whip a child unmercifully or bang him against the wall or in some other way abuse him. They are taking out their unhappiness on a child who cannot fight back or protect himself.

Unregenerate Nature

People are wonderful. They can love, forgive, do great things, and be kind in a thousand ways. But by nature, all human beings are sinners. We read in Romans 3:23: "For all have sinned and fall short of the glory of God." Our forebears, Adam and Eve, chose to sin in the Garden of Eden, and as a result, the blight of sin has come upon the entire human race. Romans 5:12 says, "Therefore, just as through one man sin entered the world, and death through sin, and thus death spread to all men, because all sinned."

The sinful nature of man is capable of every evil thing. We don't have to prove this; all we need to do is look around to witness it. In every aspect of life, man's unregenerate nature rears its ugly head.

It is second nature for people to do the wrong thing. Much abuse to children can be traced directly to a mother or father who does not know Christ and is not being led by God's Holy Spirit. This is one of the greatest causes of child abuse.

Hidden Problems

Some children have hidden problems. They may be nice looking and normal in nearly every way. Still they have very serious problems causing them to act in undesirable ways. So often, mothers and dads would never suspect that their child has a hidden problem, such as hearing loss or low blood sugar or a low IQ level. Through the years I have found that a child's misbehavior may be caused by poor nutrition, or the child may have undetected mild brain damage.

I have known parents who tried in vain to get their child to obey. Believing that the child was stubborn, they whipped him. When the parents finally came to me for help, I gave the child psychological tests and found that he had a rather low IQ and could not understand what the teachers at school or the parents at home wanted. Christian professionals can diagnose and determine precisely what the problem is, how it came about, and what should be done to resolve it. This child's suffering could have been alleviated if the parents had brought him in sooner.

If parents have a child who exhibits behavior they cannot understand or control, they would be wise to seek professional help before the situation worsens. Their child may have one of these hidden problems.

Inflexibility

One of the finest assets a parent can have is flexibility. He is able to stop in the middle of almost any activity and do so happily. He can shift gears suddenly. That's what raising children is all about. Kids are active and unpredictable. One minute they may be peacefully watching a TV program, the next minute they may be climbing up in the cupboards to get the cookies and peanut butter, and the next moment they may be running into the house carrying a dead frog or a live one!

What does a parent do? An effective parent takes all these things in stride during the day. He's flexible enough to carry on his own interests and activities and at the same time bend sufficiently to meet the needs of the little children and teenagers in the home.

Many parents aren't flexible because of their basic insecurity and hostility. They have to have everything in life lined up nicely and neatly, and they don't want anyone to rattle their cage. As long as activities go along in a rather uniform, predictable manner, they can manage. But when emergencies and unexpected activities come along, they lose their poise, fly off the handle, and often strike out at the nearest person. They lack an important balance. They are unable to be both flexible and organized.

Depressed Conditions

Depressed conditions cause many hardships and family problems. When a parent is unemployed and there is little or no income, every member of the family feels it. The father is discouraged and often angry; the mother is distraught and upset; the children cry and complain. In other words, the entire family is frustrated and on edge.

It is only natural that during these times when there is inadequate financial income, and when families are having to live in poverty, that tempers flare and abuse results. Children may fight more than ordinarily; parents may hurl accusations at each other; and the big ones (the parents) may take it out on the little ones (the children).

Church members and other people in the community should be aware of such depressed conditions. Otherwise children will grow up with abusive scars that are hard to erase and they may eventually replicate this behavior in their own homes.

If we were to study a thousand parents who were having trouble with their children, we would find many of them to be rigid and unbending. Rigid parents usually respond to problems with severe threats, unreasonable discipline, or outright abuse.

The young and impressionable—our children—are too precious for us to allow their abuse to continue. The points discussed in this chapter should serve to heighten our awareness of specific aspects of the problem and alert us to ways of identifying possible abuse. Any efforts that we can make to curtail this problem will have beneficial effects on both present and future generations. Although it is no guarantee of easy sailing, a godly heritage makes a difference throughout life, as we shall see in the next chapter.

Understanding the Golden Years

When you're sitting in church have you ever looked around and noticed how many people are in their sixties, seventies, and eighties? You wouldn't have seen many thirty years ago, but now the number of senior citizens is climbing up the population charts.

At the turn of the century only 4 percent of America's population was over sixty-five years of age. In fact, it was quite common for only a small percentage to live to see their firstborn get married. People just didn't live that long.

Things have changed markedly today. With medicine's advances in treating arteriosclerosis, heart disease, and cancer, many seniors are reaching their eighties and nineties. Indeed, in 1984, 11.7 percent of America's population had reached sixty-five or over. That means nearly twenty-six million Americans are in their golden years and are eligible for retirement. If parents are to be at their best, they must not only think of "other" people's getting older; they must also give thought to the fact that *they* are becoming older, too.

The latest census shows a drastic change taking place in the make-up of American society. For the first time in our history, our population has more people over sixty-five than it has teen-agers. How startling! More people are living in retirement in this country than are sitting in our high school classes.

This population change is showing its muscle and power

throughout our culture. In politics, for example, government officials or would-be politicians no longer make college campus visits their number one priority. Instead, they look for senior citizen groups and functions, because that is where more of the votes (and money) are.

Television is also reflecting the change. More commercials geared for the older adult are coming into our living rooms and more "elderly" actors are appearing on the screen and gaining national notoriety. The best example is the little woman in the hamburger commercials who had the entire country shouting, "Where's the beef? Where's the beef?"

When we think of older people, we may picture them sitting in rocking chairs on a lawn outside a nursing home, but that's no longer true. Only 4 percent of those who are sixty-five or older require institutional care.

Many older people are extremely active. They participate in many activities of churches and organizations. Some of them are heads of state or heads of major companies. They are attacking life vigorously, traveling and taking advantage of all life has to offer them.

A Time of Gains

A few days ago I heard a specialist on aging say, "Old age is a season of losses." This statement is only partially true. That's like saying a star is something in the sky. True, it is in the sky, but it is a lot more than "something." The latter years are much more than a time when a person is experiencing losses. It is also a time of gains!

We do tend to lose our strength, our ability to move fast, and our ability to remember easily, but the senior years may be described as a season of wisdom and experience. It is a time when a person may be gathering years of understanding so that he can make excellent decisions and avoid many mistakes. It is a time when he can give wise counsel to those who have not yet traveled that way or that far.

The senior season is also one of spiritual fulfillment. Naturally, the person must have been walking with the Lord, trusting Christ, growing through the Word, and serving God. Even though we were once blinded by our own sin, God can give us light and lead us graciously throughout life.

> I will bring the blind by a way they did not know;
> I will lead them in paths they have not known.
> I will make darkness light before them,
> And crooked places straight.
> These things I will do for them,
> And not forsake them (Isa. 42:16).

Praise God this is true.

Too Old to Change?

"A child is like a soft piece of clay; he's so pliable, so easy to mold." This statement is basically true. But does it imply, then, that elderly people are like cement, so difficult to change?

Let me share my experiences with counseling older people. Each year my staff and I hold a week's conference at Lake Yale, Florida, which we call "Florida in February." It is attended by Christians from across the nation, including young married couples, business people, "snow birds," and others. In 1980 we began to add a new dimension by offering group psychological tests and group counseling as well as individual Christian counseling.

The first year I was sure the middle-aged and young people would want counseling. But I wondered if the retired people would take the tests and get into counseling each day. Much to my pleasure, they did. White-haired men and women would take the tests, show up the next morning for an interpretation of their test results, and then come each day for small group counseling.

Since I led a small therapy group each day, I noted the response of the older people to professional diagnosis and counseling. I found that the older ones got just as much from the counseling sessions as any of the others. They took their test findings and diagnoses seriously. They wanted to talk about their scores, and they were eager to begin therapy to bring about significant changes in their lives.

By the end of the week they had gained many insights, they had discussed the causes of their behavior, they had begun to feel differently about themselves, and they had begun to change.

This experience at Lake Yale paralleled other experiences I've had at the counseling center at the Narramore Christian Foundation Campus. Many people of retirement age (along with thousands of younger people) have come for counseling, and we have seen tremendous changes in their lives.

Yet I know that not many older people are going anywhere for counseling. Less than 3 percent of those under treatment by clinics or private therapists are sixty-five or older. Although they account for nearly 12 percent of the population, and although they are twice as likely to be hospitalized for mental disorders, very few seek psychotherapy.

The average sixty-five year old can expect to live fifteen or twenty additional years. What happens to them between sixty-five and eighty-five? Many face a new set of problems, such as less physical energy, greater risk of illness, failing memory, a diminished ability to think quickly, the impact of serious illnesses, death of loved ones, loss of friends, and moves to new locations and churches. Adjustments to such problems could be greatly enhanced by counseling. Why, then, are the elderly not turning to counselors for help?

One reason is that most professional therapists are not actively seeking such clients. Nearly 70 percent of clinical psychologists report they are not treating *any* older patients. Many mental health professionals agree with Freud, who wrote it is inappropriate to try to treat older patients (whom he defined years ago as people beyond fifty).

Counselors often feel it is more important to help young people who have their entire lives ahead of them. Today's young crop of counselors may not understand older people; consequently, they may not feel comfortable with them.

Another reason is the reluctance of elderly people to seek help. They have grown up at a time when there was considerable stigma attached to psychotherapy. Perhaps you remember a candidate for vice-president of the United States who was forced to step down when word got out that he had once been in therapy! It is exceedingly difficult for such people to admit the need for counseling help.

But the need often exists. Many elderly people could cope more successfully with their difficult problems if they had the help of professional counselors. The ever-increasing number of the elderly in our country should cause mental health professionals to address themselves more actively to meeting these needs.

Older people *can* change, and they can change remarkably. I have seen this through first-hand experience. They will respond unusually well if they are given an opportunity for group or private counseling. Quite naturally, success in professional counseling is much the same as with any other age group. It depends upon the client's desire to change, proper diagnosis, the severity and nature of the problem, the counselor's skill as a therapist, what the client has going for him, and the application of God's Word to the problem.

The Question of the Live-in Parent

Although most senior citizens do not require institutional care, they may still face the problem of deciding where to live. The family home may require more upkeep than they are able or willing to devote to it. Or the cost of keeping a large home may be prohibitive. Or one spouse may die, leaving the other one alone and unable to cope. If they decide to move from their present location, where will they go? Where is the most desirable place for people to live when they become older?

Actually there are many more choices today than in previous years. Many organizations, church denominations, and other groups are providing alternatives, such as cluster homes, condominiums, and similar group arrangements.

How about living with one's children? Such a solution may be good in some instances, but it may not always be the best choice. Let's explore some of the reasons why.

The Joneses' drive home from the Sunnyside home was unusually somber one Sunday afternoon. Bob's mother had been in the rest home for several months now, and though Bob and Shirley had visited quite regularly, they had never felt so down. Then again, Mom had never come straight out and asked before. Oh, she had hinted several times previously, but today she just blurted it out: "I don't see why I can't come live with you and the boys."

Shirley finally had to interrupt the silence that had dominated the car, "Oh, Bob, I don't know what to do."

"There's nothing we can do," Bob shrugged. "You know we weighed all the facts before she moved there. There's no way we could care for her and three growing boys."

"I know," Shirley choked, "and I try to tell myself that this is the best for her and us, but I just feel so guilty! Terribly guilty."

Certainly, neither this conversation nor this situation is unique. Chances are, you have faced or will face this problem of how to care for an elderly parent. It has become a common concern, creating much hostility and guilt within families.

If you haven't dealt with this problem yet, perhaps you know some friends or people in your church who have. Have you shaken your head, wondering why a certain couple has put their aging father or mother in the rest home, rather than having him or her live with them? Have you passed judgment on them for doing so?

It is a situation and decision that is often tragically misunderstood, and perhaps we should not be so quick to judge. The truth is that there are several reasons why it may *not* be best for the elderly parent to live with the son's or daughter's family.

Yes, it is a biblical principle that we should love and care for our parents, but there are times when having them live in our home is not the best type of love and care we can give. Here are several reasons why it may not be wise to have the parents live in your home. Perhaps you'll find that the guilt or judgment you feel inside is not of God.

1. *There has been a long-standing personality conflict between the elderly parent and the son or daughter.* Jenny waited twenty years before she moved away from home. For as long as she could remember, her life had been one continuous shouting match. Her mother was always overly critical. In her mother's eyes, Jenny could do nothing right, and her mother always told her so. As Jenny became older, she began shouting back. The day she moved out, they had the biggest argument of all. Now, with her father dead and her mother getting older, her mother wants to move in with her.

Jenny knows that nothing has changed since she was a teen-ager. She may have given up trying to outshout her mother, but those same feelings of hostility and frustration are there every time she hangs up the phone.

How could these two women manage to live together? Such personality clashes are serious problems, often requiring professional help. Whatever the reason for the conflict, Jenny is probably wise not to have her mother move in until the problem is faced and resolved. Having these two women living together would not benefit either one. In fact, it could easily destroy both lives.

2. *The live-in older person may have a negative influence on the grandchildren.* Grandfather is a non-Christian who raised his children in an ungodly home. His son, however, accepted Christ and married a Christian woman, and they are raising their children in a manner pleasing to God. Now Grandfather wants to live with his son and his family.

An outsider's response might be, "What a chance to witness to this man! Let him see how God lives in his son's home day after day, and surely the grandfather will become a Christian."

This couple has been praying for and witnessing to Grandfather for years, but he has chosen not to trust the Lord. He still drinks heavily and swears without thought. Such behavior could have a bad influence on the grandchildren, and the couple realizes that it would be bad to have Grandfather around the children every day.

In addition, the couple has to consider Grandfather's other morals and vices. How does he view women and sex? What type of counsel is he going to give a teen-ager on how to live those "discovery" years? Will he be the dominating personality in the household, having the final say and dictate "the way things are"? Will he accuse his son of disrespect when he is challenged? How will the children see this—Dad being disobedient to Grandfather?

It's important to consider these factors, especially since

Grandfather has a strong, hostile personality. The couple should not cease praying for him, but as parents, they must remember their God-given responsibility for the children.

3. *The mother or father may be extremely anxious and unable to handle the situation.* It is not unusual to find that a couple, no matter how young, is barely getting through each day. Nora, for example, is a young mother who is extremely anxious. Nearly everything that happens bothers her. Whatever she does seems to have some anxiety attached to it. She has a very low frustration threshold. She can barely stand to have the kids play in the house. Yet she is nervous when they are outside and worries about what is happening to them.

Her husband does everything he can to calm her down and help her. But sometimes it's just too much, and he loses his usual cool and tells her off.

Nora's mother has a serious thyroid condition, and Nora herself has been treated for the same thing. She was an exceptionally nervous child. Now marriage and several kids are almost too much.

How about her husband's mother or father moving in with her? Common sense dictates that it is certainly not wise. Nora can hardly live with herself, much less someone else who may be critical and demanding.

4. *The house is too small.* If only the house were bigger, you would have no hesitation in asking Mom to live with you. But God has not seen fit to provide a bigger home, and such physical and material circumstances must be considered before asking Mom to move in. Material limitations must be considered.

In your small house, the three boys share one bedroom, and you and your spouse have the other. Having the kids sleep in the living room so Grandma can have the bedroom would be a strain on the kids and possibly a discomfort to an overly sympathetic grandmother. Such a move could cause resentment on the children's part and guilt on the grand-mother's.

5. *One of the spouses doesn't want the aged person there.* Jim doesn't like his mother-in-law, Ann is afraid of her father-in-law, or Jenny just can't get along with her mother. Whatever the reason, in some cases one spouse just doesn't want to share the couple's home with the aged parent. These feelings can be very deep and complex, requiring a not-so-simple solution. In the meantime, it would be unwise to force the aged parent into this situation where he or she is not wanted and is told so.

Not only is there the risk of further damaging the relationship between the unwilling spouses and the parent, but there is also the chance of ruining the marriage. "If your mother moves in, I move out!" A married couple's first responsibility is to each other. They are one flesh in God's eyes, and their wedding vows were made not only to each other but to Him as well.

6. *It would cause a financial hardship.* Perhaps the family is just getting by, living from paycheck to paycheck. The addition of an extra person to the family would be financially impossible.

Even families that are living comfortably—having enough extra income to pay for Johnny's braces or the station wagon's repairs—may find a live-in grandfather costly, especially if he is ill. Perhaps he needs numerous types of pills or canisters of oxygen for his emphysema. The cost of weekly trips to the specialist can exceed the coverage of insurance. The cost of health care is an important consideration and must be viewed realistically.

7. *The family is unable to handle required medical care.* Beyond the problem of cost, a family must consider the administering of medical care—the who, what, when, where, and how of it.

Grandmother's heart condition makes surgery for the gallstones impossible. The doctor prescribes shots for the pain. Who's going to give them? Will that person be available at all times, since the attacks can happen at any time? Or perhaps she is incontinent. Is someone physically able and available to wash her and change her sheets?

It takes a special person to do a nurse's job and not everyone is physically or emotionally capable of doing it. Families must seriously weigh their capabilities.

8. *The older live-in person may have a tendency toward molestation.*

CAROL: Honey, I just don't think it's a good idea to have your father come live with us right now. I don't think it would be good for Lori.

DOUG: Lori? Why not for Lori? Dad loves to see her. She's the only grandchild he has.

CAROL: Well, you know, the last few times I've taken her to him for baby-sitting, she's cried and fought like you wouldn't believe. And yesterday when we stopped by to see him, she stuck to me like glue. She wrapped herself around my leg and wouldn't let go, even when I went into the kitchen or out for the mail.

DOUG: That's unusual. Was she frightened?

CAROL: I think so. Then there was that dream she had last night. You didn't hear her until she started crying, but she was talking in her sleep. It sounded like she was saying, "No Papa, don't. It hurts."

DOUG: Carol, you don't think that Dad would hurt Lori, do you? She's only three—his own granddaughter.

CAROL: I know...I know. I've tried to ask her, but she doesn't understand, and she seems afraid to talk about it.

A shocking situation, one that is very difficult to accept. Yet, if there is solid suspicion that Grandpa may molest the children, then he shouldn't move in with the family. If possible, wait until the truth can be learned. The children's safety must be the first priority.

9. *A child in the family requires special attention.* A child that is hyperactive or suffering from a neurological impairment may require much attention. Or, a child who is blind, deaf, or emotionally or mentally handicapped requires an extraordinary amount of love and time. Even children with learning disabilities demand special parental attention.

If you have such a child, you must ask yourself whether it is fair and feasible to have Grandma live in the spare room. Will you be able to give all the attention she demands and still provide adequate care for Johnny? Will he accept the fact that someone else in the house needs attention, or will he be jealous and hostile? What about you? Can you fulfill all the demands these two will put on you and still fill your role as a wife or husband and any other outside responsibilities you may have? The idea of trying to keep everyone happy while avoiding a nervous breakdown is no light matter. How much attention can you afford to give?

10. *Both spouses work.* Like most couples today, both John and Mary work outside the home. They have to in order to make house payments. Grandma has broken her hip once, and though now recovered, she's "tipsy," to say the least. There's the fear that she will fall again. It isn't safe to leave her alone.

But who would be with her if she moved in with John and Mary? Their thirteen-year-old son loves Grandma, but he's a teen-ager busy with school, football, church, and growing up. His parents don't feel right burdening him with this responsibility. Their nine-year-old daughter is willing to help, but she's not physically strong enough to help Grandma in and out of chairs. Both children would be helpless if Grandma should slip in the shower.

If Grandma were able to care for herself, then she would be happy living on her own, but she's not able and she needs constant supervision. John and Mary know that she will not get proper care at their home and, therefore, hesitate to move her in.

When it comes time for you to face the question of the live-in parent, I hope these points will help you in evaluating the situation. Prayerful consideration will lead you to the right answer.

For those who have already struggled through this decision, the bottom line is this: You needn't feel guilty for not having your parent (or parents) move in. You may have to tenderly and patiently explain your choice, then reaffirm your love in other ways. You may have to enlighten some critical friends by giving them the facts and telling them that you and God have settled the matter. If you have examined all the possibilities and prayed to God for His wisdom, and you have based your decision upon His leading, then you have undoubtedly done what is right in His sight.

The Tarnished Years

Instead of enjoying their golden years, many senior citizens will spend their remaining years feeling unwanted. Their children, grandchildren, or family members may have even told them this by outright statements or by not-so-subtle-actions. Such treatment is not what God had in mind, when Paul wrote: "Children, obey your parents in the Lord, for this is right. 'Honor your father and mother,' which is the first commandment with promise; 'that it may be well with you and you may live long on the earth'" (Eph. 6:1–3).

Mrs. Andrews was in her early seventies when her husband George died, and she had no one to depend on for encouragement and support except her son Michael.

Within a few years, Mrs. Andrews began slowing down. She only picked at her food. She seemed eager to turn over the management of her home to Michael because she felt little interest in carrying on with her own affairs.

Michael had other things in mind. As soon as his mother handed over control of her home and finances to him, he began siphoning off money from her savings, which he had made into a joint account. As Mrs. Andrews surrendered to her depression, Michael frequently "fixed" her meals of ice cream, her favorite, or cold sweetened cereal. Eventually, Mrs. Andrews had to be placed in a nursing home. Now a happy Michael can have full sway with the house and the money.

God's heart must break each time this happens, and Mrs. Andrew's heart broke as well after she was institutionalized and Michael seldom visited her.

I have a Christian friend, an elderly woman, who lives in her large, comfortable home. Since it's so spacious and because she loves her daughter, she lives in an area upstairs, and she lets her daughter and son-in-law occupy the entire downstairs as her guests.

Each evening they have dinner together in the downstairs dining room. Around six o'clock this lovely woman goes down to the first floor for their evening meal.

On one particular evening she went down a little early, and she heard her son-in-law talking to his wife in the kitchen.

"I wonder how much longer she'll live?" he asked. "I wish the old bat would kick the bucket so we could take over this house, sell it, take the money, and move to Florida. I wonder what's keeping her going. She should have died long ago!"

"When I heard him say that, I was crushed," my friend told me. "I knew he was self-centered and greedy, but when he said that, I felt so bad, so terribly, terribly bad." Then she broke down and cried.

These awful incidents are becoming more common. In every community there are senior citizens who know they are not wanted or appreciated. They're considered a burden and a nuisance. How heartbreaking it must be to reach the last years of your life and know that the people around you feel that they would be better off if you didn't exist!

Approximately one out of every twenty-five of the nation's senior population (sixty-five years of age and older) will be abused at least once during their retirement years, says Diane W. Bartchy, M.A., director of the Homemaker Program for Family Service of Long Beach, California. "Women are truly the new pioneers in a new era of American history," Bartchy adds. "Never before have there been so many elderly women in the entire history of this country. The average age for widowhood in America is fifty-six. And 85 percent of all wives outlive their husbands—and 25 percent of all women over sixty-five who live alone live in poverty."

Through her research, Bartchy learned the poverty rate for older women is 65 percent higher than for older men, and as of 1984, there were approximately 2.8 million elderly women living in poverty. What this points to, Bartchy says, is that poor elderly women are frequently a financial drain on their families. If these families are uncharitable, unchristian, and unloving, these elderly women are prime victims of abuse and neglect.

Some elderly women living alone eat cat food or cookies and potato chips because they're cheap and filling. Many elderly parents living with their children are pacified with ice cream, chocolates, and other junk foods to keep them happy, says Bev Gish, project coordinator for the Senior Multi-Purpose Center in San Gabriel, California.

Other seniors are simply neglected and ignored, and their most private physical needs are left unattended. "When you visit an elderly friend, notice if she is wearing the same clothes as last week—or last month," says Gish, referring to one woman who was never bathed and who lived on breakfast cereal and ice cream. "Is there anything in the refrigerator?"

How can this kind of neglect take place? According to Gish and other gerontologists, senior abuse is caused by several things. Some can be more clearly defined than others, and sometimes multiple reasons work together to create an abusive situation. Let's look at examples of what might happen in some homes.

Mrs. Smith, seventy-five, is being taken care of by her children because the family is unable to afford full-time nursing care. At first, Mrs. Smith's presence in the house was a real joy, her daughter told social workers, because "Grandmother" helped out with preparing meals and enjoyed baby-sitting her grandchildren.

But a few strokes changed this pleasant scene. Suddenly, almost overnight, Mrs. Smith—the self-sufficient grandmother who actually contributed to her family's well-being—became a time-consuming burden. Grandmother started losing bladder control.

Eventually, as senility took over and her brain received less and less of the oxygen it needed, Mrs. Smith began taking off her nightie at inappropriate times and frequently resorted to throwing her food. One day, when her daughter was weary of taking care of her ever-demanding mother, a food-throwing incident triggered a "blow up" and she struck and injured her mother.

Relatives may become exasperated with the day-to-day care of an elderly parent, and their frustration is compounded because the twenty-four-hour care never ends.

Furthermore, no recognition by the government is given to relatives who spend significant sums of money to care for elderly parents at home.

However, there is no excuse for parental abuse. The Bible says, "He who mistreats his father and chases away his mother/Is a son who causes shame and brings reproach" (Prov. 19:26). Clearly, parental abuse is contrary to God's Word.

Another situation that sets the stage for abuse occurs when single adults live at home with their parents or grandparents and seek ways to feed a dependency on drugs or alcohol. All too frequently, these children make verbal threats, talk their parents out of financial assets set aside for retirement, and spend the money on their habit.

Erma, seventy-eight, is a widow who has made herself dependent on her grandson Tommy. This grandson, however, has "borrowed" her credit cards on numerous occasions and has purchased hundreds of dollars worth of items in her name. Erma frequently complains about Tommy's borrowing to the police, and her last complaint led police to arrest Tommy for theft. Tommy was actually purchasing goods, then pawning them for drug money.

Abuse also occurs when the husband dies, leaving the wife a widow. A substantial number of widows are victimized by their children after their husbands pass away. The mother never established her own authority when her children were growing up, and she is easily pushed around by children and grandchildren when there is no one left to speak for her.

The Bible says, "A foolish son is a grief to his father,/And bitterness to her who bore him" (Prov. 17:25). Elderly parents who are cast off by their children and grandchildren feel intense grief and bitterness because the love they invested in their children is never returned. Many grown children are selfish and greedy, and they refuse to repay this special debt of love. They cause untold heartbreak to their aging parents who are often dependent on their children for emotional and financial support.

"Parent battering is the big problem confronting family-care professionals today," says Suzanne Steinmetz of the University of Delaware. When experts study the problem of abuse of the elderly, they can identify several factors at work:

Lack of Support

Mark and Diane live near her mother. After Diane's mother broke her hip and required several months of care, she came to live for a while with them. But none of Diane's brothers or sister offered to help, either through providing care or through paying bills. Diane felt all alone and put upon by the rest of the family.

"I never meant to hit Mom," Diane confided to her social worker. "I was so tired and discouraged. I guess I just got so infuriated after my two brothers and one sister said they wouldn't take Mom. I've had to quit my job and stay home with her. I got so mad at the whole situation that I just lashed out at her."

Mark and Diane need emotional support from their friends and financial help from the rest of the family. All too often, however, one son or daughter is left with the burden of caring for elderly parents.

Lack of Knowledge

"Parent abuse is a widespread problem that no one is talking about," says Denis Madden, director of the Clinical Research Program for Violent Behavior at the University of Maryland Medical School. As a result, many abusive children feel they are the only ones "victimized" by caring for an elderly, demanding parent.

One solution to this problem, a noted social worker says, is to join a self-help group or start one of your own. "Just by hearing that others are going through the same griefs and angers with their parents as you are will help you deal with your own frustrations."

Lack of Love

Perhaps there is no problem so devastating as the lack of love being shown for parents. A counselor in St. Louis told a reporter: "I've never seen anything like it. These kids [abusing their parents] show no remorse. They aren't a bit sorry. Are we raising a generation without conscience?"

Love plays a very important part in any relationship, but especially with aging parents who question their own adequacy and self-worth. Signs of love are absolutely necessary to a senior's well-being. A visit, a back rub, a hug and kiss, or thoughtful gesture can really brighten their day and make them feel worthy as persons.

As Christians, we know that the commandment "Honor your father and mother" (Exo. 20:12) is the first commandment with promise. Any abuse of elderly parents is totally inconsistent with what we know to be true. We owe it to all our senior citizens, not just our parents, to make sure that their golden years are golden. As in the case of child abuse, we should be alert to possible cases of abuse of the elderly. Senior citizens' worth as persons should be affirmed and reaffirmed, and their latter years should be satisfying and spiritually fulfilling ones.

8

The Powerful Persuaders

"Bang! Bang! Gotcha!" eight-year-old Tommy shouts as he surprises his friend while playing cowboys and Indians. "Hey, I know. I'll be the sheriff like in the movie we saw last night."

"Okay," Johnny agrees with sparkling eyes. "But first be the deputy so I can shoot you, then you can be the sheriff and shoot me."

"All right," Tommy says. He turns his back to Johnny, who then grabs him from behind and sticks his gun into Tommy's back.

"Bang! Bang! Bang!" Johnny yells.

Tommy falls and watches Johnny race away, then Tommy pulls out his sheriff's badge and realistic pistol and starts the chase.

Scenes like this seem innocent enough. After all, little boys have been playing cowboys, soldiers, or policemen for as long as most of us can remember. Yet such scenes give an unsettling reflection of our society.

Television

Tommy and Johnny bring to light the influence of the media on our children, especially in the realm of violence.

After a year of intensive hearings the attorney general's Task Force on Family Violence indicated that because of this country's respect and constitutional guarantee for freedom of speech, there has been a reluctance to impose censorship on the media. Little has been done to curtail the amount and types of violence depicted on television and movies, in books and magazines. In fact, recent research shows that violence in the media is increasing. In fact, recent research notes that violence is learned behavior, and the media significantly changes attitudes toward violent acts.

Every skilled teacher knows that there are many ways to teach people. A teacher can speak to a class, hoping they will understand and learn. Or a teacher can distribute a printed page to each student, expecting the eye gate to bring about comprehension.

We learn by seeing, hearing, smelling, tasting, and touching—or any combination of these. The more ways a teacher uses to reach a person, the more likely he is to learn.

One of the most powerful ways to teach a person is through television. Through this medium, people are learning through both seeing and hearing. But it doesn't stop there. The movement and action on a TV screen are aids to communication. In addition, color is especially impressive. People tend to remember color better than black and white.

Television uses another technique: the action of human beings. You may see a beautiful young woman or a crippled elderly man or a streetwise young man. People are nearly always on the screen, and nothing attracts people like other people.

TV has still another thing going for it. Each program is carefully planned by specialists to reach out and capture the viewer's attention.

Little wonder then that a commercial organization may spend millions of dollars each week on television advertising in order to sell its product. If it weren't doing the job, the company surely wouldn't dish out the dough.

Television can be used for good, but it seems the negative influences may be overwhelming.

One negative influence of television is the creation of violent and sinful acts which fill the minds of adults as well as children.

Researchers who study the frequency of television violence tell us that it rose from five acts per hour in December 1980 to almost seven violent acts per hour in May 1981. In other words, in a six-month period violence jumped 40 percent per hour. A recent report showed that the summer 1985 television season proved to be one of the most violent in the history of broadcasting. The number of times in which programs showed violent incidents skyrocketed by 68 percent over 1981. The average hour of prime time programming in late 1983 contained nearly ten cases of violence.

Dr. C. Everett Koop, surgeon general of the United States, recently said, "By the age of 18 a young person could have witnessed over 18,000 murders on television. This does not count the documentation of violence that seems to be in every television news report."

Does television cause violence? It is definitely a related factor. Studies show that people become hardened to, and immune to, such things as cruelty by watching it on television. Also, we know that some people imitate violence that they have seen on television. Indeed, the media affects the way Americans and all other people live. Consequently, it is partially responsible for the level in our homes and on our streets.

"Go for it," shrilled Ronnie, nine, an avid fan of Saturday morning cartoons. "Come on! Come on!" he wildly cheered, as one character punched, socked, and stomped on another character.

He's so cute, thought his mother, watching his antics from the kitchen. *He really gets into his cartoons.*

What she doesn't realize is that Ronnie isn't just getting into cartoons; he's getting into violence. Instead of learning about compassion and caring, Ronnie is being tutored in hostility, violence, and revenge.

A recent Gallup poll also learned that 67 percent of the public desired a ban on violent TV programs until ten o'clock at night.

Would the networks pay attention to what the public wanted? No. They wanted violence even though the public didn't want it.

Another interesting fact is that children who watch violence on television are much less likely to stop children who are fighting and hurting one another. But children who do *not* watch television are likely to stop fights and prevent children from hurting one another. In short, boys and girls who watch a great deal of television become desensitized to robbing, maiming, hurting, and killing people.

In 1982, the California Commission on Crime Control and Violence Presention published a well-documented handbook. The report made this statement, "Children spend more time watching television than in pursuing any other single activity. Even children at the lower end of the TV use spectrum—two-and-one-half hours of viewing per day—will spend more time in front of a television set by the time they are 18 years of age than in the classroom."

Research studies show that adults spend about 40 percent of their free time watching television. Television viewing ranks third in their time consumption; going to work and sleeping rank first and second. Violence does not occur on small unimportant programs. Sixty percent of the major prime time television stories use violence as conflict and solution.

Why do TV journalists report such a large number of stories with a violent content? One major reason is because they believe that violent stories have more public appeal. As a result, these reporters are helping the cause of violence because of their selfish interests.

If you have ever sat in front of a television on Saturday morning, I'm sure you've been amazed at the large number of violent cartoons. Some of these cartoons average sixty-four acts of violence per hour—more than one violent act per minute!

We may say this about viewing television violence: garbage in, garbage out. We are to a great extent what we have been watching and hearing. And if our minds have been engulfed in anger, hitting, screaming, yelling, and killing, then that's how we begin to think and act. Violence in, violence out!

Television is one of the most effective ways to teach people, and people around the world, including Americans, are getting large doses of cerebral pollution each day. What a contrast our daily diet of television is to what God says we should do: "And be kind to one another, tenderhearted, forgiving one another, just as God in Christ also forgave you" (Eph. 4:32). We'll never succeed in limiting problems in the family until we change television or stop watching the programs filled with violence and other negative influences.

At one time many people believed that television hostility had a cathartic effect on the viewer. They thought that a person's hostile energy was drained off by seeing and identifying with angry and violent people on TV. But today we know from research that this is not true. Watching violence on TV doesn't drain off anyone's anger and hostility. It only confirms that hostility and says, "Go ahead and be angry. Shoot 'em up if you want to."

Researchers have found that even a look at "justified violence" (getting even with criminals) increases the likelihood and severity of children's use of violence against children they dislike. The idea that crime doesn't pay doesn't come across. The main message that sticks with them is, "Hurt 'em if you feel like it."

Violence on TV teaches people that violence is an acceptable way to feel and act. This principle applies to nearly everything people see and hear on television. Viewers tend to think that whatever they see on TV is acceptable in society. If it is not acceptable now, it is the "coming thing."

As concerned as I am about the violence shown on television, I'm equally concerned about a more subtle influence: the general secular and godless lifestyle portrayed.

Only a few nights ago I was watching the evening news. Just before it went off I fell asleep. About twenty minutes later I woke up and saw that a "highly rated" show had come on. What cursing and swearing were coming out of the TV! I was shocked. I turned off the set and sat there nearly stunned for several minutes. That filthy language in my living room! I was raised on a ranch with five brothers. We roped steers and broke horses, but we never said or heard anything at home like the foul talk that was coming out of my television.

You can hardly watch a major program without viewing fornicators and adulterers. And they brag about their sinful living. "Are you married?" the TV host asks his guest. "Oh, no," she responds. "Bob and I just live together."

"Do you like it better that way?" he questions.

"We sure do," she says. "No contracts."

So they laugh and make fun of things pure and good. They despise God's eternal Word. They don't know how obnoxious they are.

Does this attitude affect people? Of course it does. We tend to live at the level of the television we watch. I know a woman, for example, who watches a soap opera each day. When one o'clock in the afternoon rolls around, she locks the front door, pulls the drapes, and takes the phone off the hook. Nothing is permitted to interrupt her daily appointment with her "soap." Even if her house were burning down, I imagine the firemen would have to pull her out of her chair! She is eating and drinking at the polluted cisterns of television.

How often do newscasters report the great Christian events of our day? Even if they know what's happening, they seldom mention it. Or if they do, they usually minimize them until great Christian events are squeezed down to little nothings. If Christ came back to earth tomorrow, I doubt if they would mention it.

When we sit in front of the TV, we rarely think of the many men and women who are involved in producing the shows. There are the stage and prop people, the writers, the lighting people, the set designers, the actors and actresses, musicians and speakers, interviewers and others. One of the major differences between a typical TV production and a Christian program is the people. Those who are responsible for producing a Christian project are born again. They live for the Lord. They desire to make everything in their project magnify Jesus Christ. They pray each day that God will use their project and lead people to Christ, to help people grow in the Lord and to live happier, more consecrated lives.

These spiritual objectives, of course, are lacking in nearly all secular TV programs. Most of the people producing secular TV are unsaved, and their final product shows it. For the most part secular TV interferes with people yielding themselves to Jesus Christ.

What biblical and spiritual instruction do you receive from secular TV? Virtually nothing. What a contrast to Christian TV!

God has a great program going on in this world, and you and I are a part of the program. Throughout America, Russia, South America, Africa, in every country there are human beings God has created. They all have a part of God's great pageant on earth.

Some are hindering the cause of Christ: others are enhancing it. God is working in unbelievable ways in the hearts of individuals around the world. Various Christian organizations are accomplishing God's will in ways that were never believed possible a few years ago.

But do you hear about it on TV? Seldom. Consequently people are getting an extremely secular view of the world.

What does the news cable and subscription television offer us? Cable started as an alternative carrier of television. Now it has grown, along with other forms of subscription television, as an alternative programmer.

The bottom line in television is money, and cable broadcasters have found they can make more of it by offering programs that airwave stations can't. At present the two biggest categories of this alternative broadcasting are sports and "mature" shows. The mature programs are more than just X-rated movies. They include racy soap operas, adult game shows, explicit talk shows, news programs, and current R-rated movies. They all create concern for the healthy, happy family.

Teen-agers make up the biggest movie-going audience in the country, even to the R-rated shows that they're not supposed to be able to enter without an adult. Now through cable, these teen-agers can watch those same cut-and-slash horror films several times a week. The films are unedited and uninterrupted. The only possible censors are the parents.

How it must grieve the heart of God who has given us the airwaves, and who has given us our minds, to see humanity using it to minimize, belittle, and blaspheme Him, their Creator.

Music

William Congreve said, "Music hath charms to soothe the savage breast, to soften rocks, or bend a knotted oak." Most of us would agree with him. The right kind of music can quiet us and make us feel at ease. It can cause us to go to sleep. It can waken and excite us. It can also put us in a good or bad mood, and it can inspire us to great heights.

Indeed, music is one of the most powerful influences in our lives. Everybody has a built-in susceptibility to music. A man once said, "If you want somebody to do something, regardless of what it is, start by having him listen to a certain type of music."

What would television advertising be like without a melody or a jingle? How dull would radio be without songs?

Music is used in hospitals to soothe people who have emotional and mental disorders. It is used by dairymen to quiet their cows. I like to think of music as coming at a person from all four directions: in front, in back, the left, and the right. These four directions are achieved through the melody, which is difficult to get out of your mind, the harmony, which brings color and warmth, the words, which give literary meaning, and the rhythm, which excites and persuades.

Music is used for good and for evil. On the radio you can locate station after station pumping hard, vulgar music at you. If you attend a contemporary music concert, you are likely to hear the same. Most best-selling recordings are no better. Such music is usually the reflection of unhappy, unfulfilled, problem-laden people. It is the language of hopelessness and confusion. I've heard this detrimental music from Africa to Alaska and from Hong Kong to Hoboken. But its message is much the same: "I'm confused." Probably few people realize the detrimental effect of the wrong kind of music upon the human mind and emotions.

There is evidence that even unborn babies are influenced by music their mothers hear. On June 7, 1983, the *Los Angeles Times* quoted Canadian psychiatrist Dr. Thomas Verny, author of *The Secret Life of the Unborn Child*, as saying,

> Rock 'n roll is particularly upsetting to the unborn child, possibly because it is so very tiny and feels threatened by the aggressive overtones of much rock music...one mother suffered a broken rib at a rock concert because of her unborn child's strenuous kicks...an obvious protest rather than a fetal show of enthusiasm for the performance in question.

> In contrast classical music, religious hymns and some folk songs appear to soothe the unborn child who is becoming increasingly aware of the environment outside the womb several months after conception.

In a society where there are so many broken homes and family problems, raucous, unsettling music abounds. Such music tends to attract unsaved, unfulfilled people, then instead of helping them, it influences them negatively.

If you want to eliminate many quarrels, hurt feelings, and problems in your family, flood your home with Christian music. It is a true power of influence.

Alcohol and Other Drugs

Many organizations across America are studying the effects of alcohol and its relationship to family problems. Volumes are being written about it, so it is not our purpose here to present detailed, definitive findings about the devastating effects of drinking. What we will examine is the seriousness of the problems caused directly or indirectly by alcohol.

Alcohol and other drugs influence people in many harmful ways. Hundreds of reports from professionals describe the detrimental effects of alcohol and other drugs on family life. The following statements and findings are just a small, typical sampling.

1. The pharmacological properties of depressant drugs, such as barbiturates and alcohol, are highly conducive to fighting, quarreling, wife abuse, child abuse, beating, and incest.

2. Chemical entities other than drugs—food, food additives, environmental pollutants, toxic metals—and vitamin deficiencies or chemical imbalances can trigger violent behavior or aggravate a pre-existing tendency toward violence in some persons.

3. When depressent drugs such as alcohol and barbiturates combine with other factors such as frequent, high-dosage use, or a volatile home or work setting, they are highly correlated with violence. Such chemical substances also cause serious behavior problems in a person who already has low self-esteem, or is rigid, compulsive, basically insecure, or has a negative, hostile personality.

4. A recent study by the New York University School of Medicine found that homicidal children were much more likely than others to have alcoholic parents.

5. There appears to be an association between abusing alcohol and other drugs and having an earlier incestuous experience. Forty-four percent of the female drug abusers in one study, and 70 percent of those in another, reported having been sexually abused by a family member.

6. Official reports indicate that alcohol-abuse is a factor in more than 60 percent of the nation's homicides. It is present in 50 percent of the rapes, up to 70 percent of the assaults, and 80 percent of the suicides.

7. The following statement quoted in the Family Violence Task Force report seems shocking, but it is not unusual. "We have over a million children in Texas who wake up in homes with at least one alcohol-addicted parent. Their

chances of being abused children are very high" (Ross Newby, alcohol abuse professional).

8. A recent study was made of one hundred women, all of whom were married to alcoholics. Seventy-two percent of them had been violently threatened. Forty-five percent of them had been beaten.

9. A Minnesota study of nearly one hundred abused wives found that 87 percent of the abusing men were alcohol abusers. Thirty-five percent were daily drinkers.

10. A report from the Austin (Texas) Family House shows that 99 percent of the women treated are second- or third-generation alcohol-addicted people themselves. Ninety-eight percent are victims of incest, and more than 90 percent have siblings who are chemically dependent. One hundred percent of the women have husbands or partners who have alcohol or drug abuse problems.

Findings like these show the magnitude of the problem. It is not surprising that more and more people are working together to combat the effects of this menace to the family— and to society.

Pornography

My first major encounter with pornography peddlers came several years ago when I was asked by the city of Los Angeles to serve as an expert witness at a pornography trial. The city attorney and his staff were trying to crack down on a particular publisher of pornographic magazines. The publisher had been cited, and the case was coming up in court. I had been chosen for my particular assignment because I was a licensed psychologist in the state, and I had written a major book on sex education, *Life and Love*. I was also a credentialed school psychologist and had been serving as a consulting psychologist on the staff of the Los Angeles

County Superintendent of Schools.

In preparation for the trial the city attorney's office asked me to meet with the deputy attorney in Los Angeles. We discussed the upcoming trial, and he handed me about a dozen pornographic books to review so I could be questioned about them in the courtroom. After glancing at a couple, I could see how absolutely degrading they were, so I quickly slipped them into my briefcase, hoping that no one who was walking by where we were sitting would recognize me as a leading Christian psychologist!

As I took them home and read them, I could see how diabolical they were. The authors were both men and women who, for the most part, could sling a pen. They were forceful writers who could lead their readers to sadistic excitement. I noted several pages in the books that I might cite in court to show how torrid and debased they were.

When I was called to the stand, our attorney asked me several questions. Then he asked me to read portions from the books and make comments on the effect such material would have on human beings. Fortunately, I had considerable training in speech and drama. So when I read a portion of my first example, I read it exactly as it was written, but I did it with all of the feelings and emphasis I could muster. As I was into my second paragraph, the attorney for the other side saw that he was confronted with more than he had bargained for. He jumped up and began to scream, "Stop, stop, stop," and the judge and those present were convinced that, indeed, the material was not fit for wild swine!

Since that time, the publishing of pornographic magazines, books, and pictures has gotten much worse. In the recent attorney's general's Task Force on Family Violence report, the committee came down hard on the effect of pornography on family violence when it said:

Pornography has become a big business in the United States. Some government officials estimate that pornography is a $4 to $6 billion industry that continues to grow and expand. It is an industry that victimizes countless children who are exploited in pornographic photographs and films. Task Force testimony indicates that an alarming number of rape and sexual assault offenders report that they were acting out behavior they had viewed in pornographic materials. Experts also testified that the only uses for child pornography are to lower the inhibitions of the child, gratify the sexual desires of the pedophile, and control and blackmail the child (page 112).

Sometimes we think of pornography publishers as a little group of vile men and women who are working in a little back room somewhere, printing their dirty little books and magazines in order to make a fast buck.

But is this an accurate picture? Is this really what's happening?

In February of 1984, attorney Bruce Taylor, vice president and counselor of the Citizens for Decency through Law, Inc., in Phoenix, Arizona, published the following statement that gets down to the nitty-gritty of the pornography industry:

For the last 15 years in America, the pornography industry in America has had a definite and devastating impact on the stability of the American family and the relationship between men and women and children. In the early 1970s, traditional organized crime families consolidated their influence and control over distributors and producers of pornographic magazines and films. By the mid-1970s, the population and international distribution of hard-core pornography was restricted to a relatively small group of men with ties to organized crime. These producers and distributors are referred to as the Pornography Syndicate and consist of film producers who are members of the Adult Film Association of America (AFAA) and an interlocking series of hundreds of corporations which are basically subsidiaries of two major distribution empires. This pornography syndicate and members of La Cosa Nostra opened hard-core pornography outlets ("adult bookstores" and "adult theatres") in every major city and hundreds of small communities. Hard-core pornography is therefore available illegally in every state and to nearly every adult in this country.

What does pornography do to a person? Does it really affect him that much? Is it something a person looks at, then dismisses from his mind? Most people don't stop to think about the real impact of pornography.

First, it causes the reader to think less of himself. As the reader looks at the sordid material transmitted from the eyes into the crevices of the brain, he identifies with one of the people on the page. He becomes either the perpetrator or the victim, and both are bad. Neither one makes him feel that he is an outstanding, godly person able to accomplish noble deeds for mankind.

Second, pornographic material causes the reader to degrade other people. He sees others in the role of debasing or being debased. Instead of thinking of human beings as worthwhile, precious people to be respected, he is lowering his view of them to little more than animals.

Third, he is degrading his view of his own mother who gave birth to him and who raised him. After all, the prostituted woman in the picture is, in a sense, his own mother. His mother is a human female, and the lewd character on the page is a female. Unconsciously, he is lowering all women to a debased status.

Fourth, the reading of pornographic literature sometimes leads to illegal and criminal behavior. Research is replete with findings regarding people who read pornographic material, then go out and duplicate the very things they read.

Our jails and penitentiaries are filled with men who have been "taught" through pornographic books and pictures.

Fifth, pornography has a special appeal to, and consequently a profound effect upon, (1) young people who want to learn and know about sex, (2) men and women who are not fulfilled sexually and who are frustrated, and (3) susceptible people who have personality maladjustments as well as those who have mental disturbances.

Finally, pornography is detrimental to a person because it doesn't offer any solutions to his problems. It gives no insights to help him understand himself better so he can change his behavior. It doesn't furnish any lofty ideals or encouragement. It only makes him stew more viciously in his own maladjustments, depression, hostility, insecurity, and paranoia.

All human beings have Adamic natures. We live under the curse of Adam and Eve. Consequently, we have a natural tendency to sin. The last thing we need is a detrimental influence such as pornography. Pornography pulls a person only one way: down.

What we *do* need is "the peace of God, which surpasses all understanding," and which "will guard [our] hearts and minds through Christ Jesus" (Phil. 4:7).

The sweet, uplifting Word of God tells us what we should be hearing, viewing, and thinking about: "Whatever things are true, whatever things are noble, whatever things are just, whatever things are pure, whatever things are lovely, whatever things are of good report, if there is any virture and if there is anything praiseworthy—meditate on these things" (Phil. 4:8).

Advocates of Abortion

My son, Kevin, and I were invited to a conference at the

White House dealing with abortion. Surgeon General C. Everett Koop spoke briefly about the issue. Then several panel members told about their success in establishing anti-abortion programs and clinics across America. I was especially interested in what they had to say because through the years I have received many letters from radio listeners and others who have told me about their tragic experiences of having an abortion. But I have never received one letter from a woman saying she was happy she had done it.

Panel after panel told about the joy and privilege of not only salvaging the lives of thousands of babies, but also preventing mothers from going through agonizing guilt and remorse because of having taken the life of an innocent child. When I returned home to my office in Rosemead, I found a letter like many others I have received that told of a woman's experience with abortion.

Dear Sir:

I recently was listening to your radio broadcast. Your discussion was on sexual sin and forgiveness that is available through God.

It touched me because of my past experience. I've felt a burden since my glorious forgiveness, to do something or say something regarding my problems, but I haven't known how to do it.

The problem concerns abortion. I had intercourse with one man in my lifetime before marriage and it resulted in pregnancy. The pregnancy was "terminated." The child was destroyed by abortion.

What I want to share is what it's like to have committed such an irreversible sin. There are 1.5 million babies murdered each year. Some of these are repeats by the same women; but surely that still leaves at least a million women who've committed murder. I'm certain that many of them realize what they've actually done and have begun to suffer the living death it brings.

I was 20 years old when I went to the university physician. There was no discussion or thought about the fact that it was a true human being inside me. I was shuffled from one person to the next and it seemed all a blur to me.

I found myself in New York met by a "lady in a pink smock" (one way to recognize abortion employees) who then led me to a van filled with other women. As I look back it was like herding cattle—a description often used to describe the murder of the Jews by Hitler.

I went through the procedure never fully realizing what was happening to that baby. He or she was being ripped to pieces within me by the suction method used.

Within six months I was married. Within a year I had a baby girl. I resented her. She made it seem as though the first murdered child was a wasted effort. As she grew up, I hated her more and more. It wasn't until she almost died from pneumonia that I realized I felt anything positive for her. She recovered from pneumonia, but she has suffered so much from my rejection. She has such deep problems.

I don't know if I can explain clearly what happened to me. My heart hardened. I laughed at times at the phrase "God is dead." That was popular in those days (1970). When I became pregnant, I felt I should get rid of the baby. I made excuses like "My mom is dying of cancer; I can't be pregnant now" or "my brother had to get married; I can't repeat that scene" or "the baby probably doesn't get a soul until after it's born, so I'm not killing any person."

I tried to cling to these excuses, but they couldn't give me peace.

As time went on in my marriage, the sexual aspect of it worsened and I hated it all. As far as I was concerned it was awful, dirty, and my husband was perverted in his desire for me. I began to hate all people.

Finally, I began to lose assurance that I was even sane. I doubted if I was mentally normal.

All through this time I left God out of my life. Once I tried to read the Bible, but it was unreadable. The words were foreign and seemed to jump around the page. I couldn't even focus on them. I cried day and night. I pushed my family away from me. I rejected friendships and became distrustful of everyone. At times I felt I was insane and thought that some day people were going to find out about me. I'd hold on to the bed to keep from falling. I knew I was going to hell—even though I had denied it existed.

Then Jesus reached out to me as I kept struggling to read the Bible. I had a red-letter edition where Jesus' words were printed in red. That's all I wanted to read, just what Jesus said.

Over a period of 2–3 years I was brought back to the Lord, was born again, and received the gifts of God's Holy Spirit. I am now a new creation in Christ Jesus. He has healed me.

So as a result of premartial sex, I committed murder, rejected God, rejected the next child, rejected my husband and everyone else, and almost lost it all to Satan.

Please, Dr. Narramore, tell the women you talk to on the radio not to abort their child. It is murder and it also destroys the mother.

Tell them the suffering can finally stop...stop now through being saved. Please do this.

Today the average person knows much more about the life of the baby before it is born than we did even a few years ago. A simple fact is that if the baby is not dead, then it's alive. If it's alive, it's growing. So a baby is both alive and growing inside the mother. Modern techniques enable a pregnant woman to lie on her back and on a screen see the movements of the tiny one inside her. Not long ago I saw this on television, and as our family sat in our living room we could see on the screen the tiny baby in the womb, only a few weeks old, scratching its elbow and sucking its thumb. Then the narrator explained that millions of babies much older than that one are aborted.

Many groups in our nation are strong advocates of abortion. The harm they cause through their position on this issue is far-reaching. Abortion brings many problems not only because of the guilt of the parent and denial of life to the tiny human beings but also because of the insensitivity and disregard toward human life. This callousness is profound. If young men and young women become calloused enough to end the life of a child, then it only follows that they will tend to have many problems in life and not hesitate to perform other acts of violence.

Homosexual Activists

Homosexual activists have had a treacherous effect on the family. In fact, they have had a harmful impact upon society in general.

Homosexuality is serious inasmuch as it represents a sick personality. Clinically speaking, it is not so much a sex problem as it is a personality disturbance. In other words, a therapist who helps a person with homosexual tendencies focuses less on the sexual symptoms and more on the person's childhood emotional deprivations and how they now affect the adult in his daily functioning.

As homosexual groups become more blatant, they also become more dangerous. They are increasingly aggressive in their search for young people they can introduce to their sinful practices. Young people who have rather low defenses can be ensnared, then left to suffer a terrible life.

Because of my radio broadcasts, televison programs, speaking engagments, and books, many people write me about their homosexual problems. The following letter is quite typical.

Dear Dr. Narramore:
I am a lonely, confused homosexual.

Doctors tell me that I must live a gay life to be happy. To do otherwise would go against the grain. But my people and friends are not gays. They hate gays. Therefore, I cannot show any outward sign of being gay. The gay world has NOT been FOR me; only against me for the most part. Gay men only like skinny, pretty men—of which I am not.

Also, I am a loser at friendship. I don't really have any friends any more. I have no job or any income at all. I am at the mercy of whomever will take me in. I don't even have a car or a home of my own.

Welfare does not give me enough to "get by." Last month I received only $27 in food stamps to live on for the whole four weeks. I have heart trouble and diabetes and related side effects because of no medical care. I fear that I will soon be overtaken with a diabetic coma or worse because I am out of medicine and have no money to buy any.

I have a bed at night. I am with some men who abuse me. Sometimes they take my food stamps and some have stolen my few personal effects. I do domestic work here for my bed. I may be gay, but I do not like having sex with people I do not care for or love.

I find that most people think that just because a man is homosexual, he likes sex anywhere and anyplace with anyone. It may be true for some, but not for me. I am a one-man lover. If I love him, I donate myself to him. I do not play the field as many homos (and straights) do.

I am on my way to skid row. I am without friends, without God, without hope.

Is there any help for a miserable guy like me?

When I think of the dignity that God gives human beings, my heart goes out to this wretched man. The causes of homosexuality are well documented. We know what causes a person to enter such an unnatural path, but a relatively small percentage of those who are engaged in this practice want help. Until a man accepts Christ as his personal Savior, he seldom wants to change. Therefore, he circulates throughout society, leaving a trail of sordid actions and destructive perversions. In recent years homosexuality activists have become a power of influence even in the classrooms and other places where young people work, live, and play.

All of these powers of influence—television, music, alcohol and other drugs, pornography, advocates of abortion, and homosexual activists—can and do bring harmful ideas and attitudes into our homes. As Christian parents we must see that our children are filled with healthy, godly ideas and attitudes. We can promote such positive views to our children and at the same time repudiate the opposing, negative ones. In this way children may "be wisely worldly," not "worldy wise," as Francis Quarles has said.

CHAPTER
9

Inside Information

We are threefold beings. A disorder in any of the three—physical, emotional, or spiritual—may seriously affect us. Indeed, many of the problems we experience are "inside problems"—inside our bodies.

My heart goes out to people who have gone to doctors for years and have spent large sums of money to get help, but their problems were never alleviated. In most cases, they were looking in the wrong direction for the problem, and they were seeking help from specialists who were treating them for the wrong thing.

My mailbox is stuffed nearly every day with letters from people who have gone to psychologists and psychiatrists but received no real help. When they finally sought help from a medical specialist and found that their problem was physiological rather than psychological, they improved almost immediately upon treatment. On the other hand, some have gone to a medical doctor for treatment of migraines only to later find that the pain was caused by emotional pressures; then psychologists were able to help them.

The same is true with spiritual problems. Some people who are suffering go to medical doctors but later find that their problem is really spiritual in nature. When they finally receive spiritual help, their problems clear up.

Problems inside our bodies can cause us to exhibit unusual or undesirable behavior. If a child has one of these problems and it is not detected at an early stage, the child's whole life can be affected. Think of the misery that can be averted if a child is properly treated while he is still a child and doesn't have to wait for help until he is an adult.

Neurological Impairments

Shortly after we completed our graduate study at Columbia University, my bride, Ruth, and I left New York City and headed for California. Within a week or so the Lord opened a position for me as a psychologist on the staff of the Los Angeles County Superintendent of Schools. In that capacity I had the privilege of traveling throughout Los Angeles County and serving various school districts. It was a great place to learn and grow and develop professionally.

As I went from school to school, I worked with children who had problems at home as well as in the classroom. I would visit a child in the classroom and talk at length with his teacher. I often visited the parents at their home. Usually, I would then give the child an intelligence test and other psychological tests. I would bring together any medical information that would help me to understand the child. Before long I noted that a high percentage of these troubled youngsters had physiological problems. Although I was looking for psychological problems, my findings would indicate that many of the children who were not getting along well in life actually had medical problems. So many of those who had problems had minimal brain dysfunction.

Somewhere along the line, prenatally, postnatally, or at birth, the child had suffered a mild neurological impairment. As a baby, he may have sustained a severe blow on the head. Or, he may have had an extremely high fever the parents were unable to control. More likely, he may have experienced a birth trauma; the mother may have been given medication too early or too heavily at the time of birth, so she relaxed and did not breath deeply. Thus, an adequate oxygen supply did not get through the brain cells of the baby, causing an atrophy of some of the cells. Sedatives (other than general anaesthetics) given to the mother during labor are transferred to the fetus and result in a less responsive newborn.

The brain of the fetus is rapidly developing during the last few weeks of pregnancy, and it is extremely vulnerable to damage from drugs and surgical procedures administered to the mother. Obstetric intervention procedures, including drugs and surgery, may increase risk of neurological injury to the infant.

Poor nutrition or substance abuse by a mother during pregnancy can affect the fetus and result in low birth weight and premature birth, as well as abnormal or retarded brain development. Both conditions are correlated with an increased probability of subsequent negative behavior.

Alcohol intake during pregnancy can lead to fetal alcohol syndrome—a condition known to cause low birth weight, irritability in infancy, and hyperactivity in childhood.When a child reaches school age, he may show various symptoms of neurological impairment. These, of course, prevent him from functioning well at home and at school.

My psychologist friend, Dr. Harold Burke, has studied many boys and girls with neurological impairments. As a result he constructed a list of behaviors frequently found in such children. He has grouped them under three headings:

Behavioral-Muscular
1. Hyperactive and restless
2. Erratic, flighty, or scattered behavior
3. Easily distracted, lacks continuity of effort and perseverance

4. Behavior goes in cycles
5. Quality of work may vary from day to day
6. Daydreaming, alternating with hyperactivity
7. Explosive and unpredictable behavior
8. Cannot seem to control self (speaks or jumps out of seat)
9. Poor coordination in large-muscle activities (games, etc.)

Perceptual-Discriminative
10. Confusion in spelling and writing
11. Inclined to be confused in number process
12. Difficulty in reading
13. Lacks a variety of responses, repeats himself in many situations
14. Upset by changes in routine
15. Confused in following directions
16. Confused and apprehensive about rightness of response; indecisive
17. Classroom comments are often "off the track" or peculiar
18. Difficulty reasoning things out logically with others

Social-Emotional
19. Demands much attention
20. Tends to be destructive, especially of the work of others
21. Many evidences of stubborn uncooperative behavior
22. Often withdraws quickly from group activities; works alone
23. Constant difficulty with others (apparently purposeless)
24. Shallow feelings for others
25. Cries often and easily
26. Often more confused by punishment

27. Seems generally unhappy
28. Often tells bizarre stories

Sometimes when I have discussed these symptoms over the radio or at public meetings, parents will react immediately. "You described my child to a T," they say. "He has many of the symptoms you listed." I suggest that parents who have a child with several of these symptoms seriously consider the advisability of seeing a neurologist for a proper examination. It has been my experience that if a child has problems along the lines of these symptoms, and they continue year after year, the youngster may very well have mild brain damage. I have found this especially true if all professional efforts to help the child have failed.

Quite naturally, when children who have a neurological impairment are diagnosed and treated, they take a new lease on life and become happier, healthier, and more successful in school. However, it is not uncommon to find husbands and wives who have carried their childhood disorders into marriage. When this couple seeks professional help and the neurological impairment is discovered and treated, they too enjoy remarkable improvement. The marriage is enhanced tremendously.

Body Chemistry

Not all physical problems are neurological. Some people have certain disorders in their body chemistry. The National Institute of Mental Health recently studied a number of physically violent men with no major psychiatric or neurological disorders. The most aggressive men showed high levels of norepinephrine, a substance in brain and spinal fluids associated with arousal aggression. Efforts are presently under way to develop an effective treatment for this kind of aggressive condition.

Body chemistry may change from one stage of life to another. Just because one has no apparent problems now does not mean that he never will. I remember one woman who used to come almost daily to my office at the Narramore Christian Foundation. She was receiving therapy at the Rosemead Counseling Service. As nearly as we could tell she had always been well adjusted and free from serious problems, but the last few years had been quite different. When she failed to respond favorably to the Christian counseling she was receiving, she asked me what she should do.

I suggested a medical evaluation by an endocrinologist. He found that she had a severe chemical imbalance. His treatment began to make a great difference in how she felt. The emotional problems that had not responded to sound Christian counseling or even to previous medical treatment began to disappear. In a letter to me she said, "I am so glad you explained that many seemingly emotional problems have a physical basis. Now that my body is working right again I feel great!"

Biological Factors

In addition to hormonal chemical imbalances, other biological factors may predispose some people toward acts of violence under certain circumstances. Abnormal or retarded mental development, brain disease or dysfunction, and certain genetic inclinations can also produce extreme behavior patterns. Individuals with minimal brain dysfunction or hyperkinesis, for example, are four to five times more likely to be arrested during adolescence than other teen-agers. They are nine times more likely to be arrested for serious and violent offenses than the average young person. Care must be taken, however, not to categorize an individual as abusive simply because he fits into such a group. These kinds of conditions may cause violent acts in some, or they may combine with other propensities to develop such a tendency in others, but it is grossly unfair to brand anyone as violent simply because he tends toward one of these physiological or mental types. What it does mean is that such a person may be more inclined toward violent behavior.

Alcohol and Other Drugs

Alcohol is the depressant drug most highly associated with violence. Jim doesn't have to read that fact in a book; he grew up with such knowledge. Whenever his father came home drunk, there was serious trouble. Jim often saw his mother beaten up. He and his brothers experienced the same fate. Alcohol is certainly a principal cause of domestic abuse in many families.

Not all inebriates are violent, however. Some are more likely to go to sleep or get sick or have some other reaction. Some people turn their violence inward and injure or kill themselves instead of someone else. This partially accounts for the high rate of suicide among alcohol-dependent persons.

Generally, alcohol is more conducive to violent behavior when combined with other factors such as frequent, high dosages of medicine or personality inadequacies such as poor ego functioning or rigid overcontrolled ego. Barbiturates also often produce abusive behavior when combined with alcohol.

One of the most dangerous violence-producing drugs is phencyclidine, commonly known as PCP. It often causes hallucinations that lead to extremely violent reactions.

Toxic Substances

Some metals, such as lead, mercury, cadmium, and aluminum, are toxic. Concentrated and prolonged exposure to them can produce a variety of psychological and physiological symptoms including nausea, fatigue, depression, irritability, hyperactivity, and learning difficulty. Fortunately, lead poisoning can be diagnosed readily and is treatable.

Childhood Emotional Deprivations

If you and I were only spirits fluttering around the room, all of our problems (if we had them) would be spiritual in nature, and the solution to our problems would be spiritual.

But that's not what we are. True, we are spiritual beings, but we are also physical beings with many potential medical problems and various medical solutions. We are also emotional, or psychological, beings. Consequently, we have emotional problems as well as solutions of a psychological nature.

A missionary kid said to me once, "I've lived in boarding schools overseas most of my life. I've had eight or ten sets of house parents. But five or six of them didn't know I existed."

Just as a child requires food, shelter, and clothing, his heart and mind cry for something else—emotional well-being. No person growing up is content only to eat, sleep, and exercise. He wants to feel that he is significant and worthwhile. There is some evidence that extreme sensory deprivation (failing to touch or hug a child) can result in retarded or abnormal brain development which, in turn, can lead to social maladjustment and violent behavior. Sensory stimulation, touch, and physical affection are important factors for healthy child development. In addition, the child must not be tormented with feelings of guilt. Yet many parents continually blame a child for all sorts of things and make him feel guilty.

The list is long. A number of basic emotional needs cry out for fulfillment. God has ordained the mother and father to meet these emotional requisites. Day by day, the parents make the child feel he is loved and respected. Chapters 5 and 6 of Ephesians give beautiful guidance to the family. They tell husbands, wives, children, fathers, mothers, servants, and masters what they should do. These words are not idle. God has made us, and He knows how we are to function. His instructions are necessary for healthful living.

If parents meet the basic emotional needs of a child, he is likely to grow up with happy, healthy feelings about himself. If these needs are not met, he will have distortions in his perceptions of other people. He will have a low self-esteem.

As parents follow the teachings of Christ, the child's basic emotional needs will usually be met. Yet some Christian homes are virtually loveless, and the child will never experience fulfillment of emotional needs.

Sometimes we wonder why a person who grew up in a churchgoing home has deep problems. The answer can often be found in the fact that although the parents may have had a knowledge of the Bible, they never lived it. So the child's life is much the same as if he had been raised in a godless, uncaring environment. I thought about this when I received the following letter from a woman raised in a loveless Christian home.

Dear Sir:

I believe that people can put up with almost any hardship growing up. But being unloved really puts a burden on them for life. There is an empty feeling in your heart. I believe God's love helps a great deal, but not altogether. I am a born again Christian and I am very glad I am. But it doesn't solve all of one's problems.

My husband is not a Christian, yet he has to be about the happiest person I know. Why? Because he was very loved as a child. And he wasn't brought up in a Christian family, just a *loving* family.

I know several women who are Christians and still have many emotional problems. In fact one is in a psychiatric hospital right now! Another one is seeing a psychologist who has asked her to stop going to church for a while, because she has been doing the same thing her parents did—criticizing, belittling and the like.

If I hadn't gone to a therapist before I was a Christian, I would never have become a believer, as I didn't even know what love was. God bless you for your work, I am sure you are doing wonders of good every day. In God's love.

If a person's basic emotional needs are not met on a regular basis in childhood, how will they be affected as an adult?

Emotional deprivation can reveal itself in many different ways in adulthood. Experts can't predict exactly how each person will be affected, but they are certain that emotional deprivation will have a negative impact.

One person may feel angry. He becomes angry at nearly everything that happens to him. It is as though everything should be handed to him because he is hostile for never having gotten true love and affection from his parents. He is resentful. Throughout life, he feels deprived and imposed upon.

Another person may develop a vivid fantasy life. Since he doesn't seem to "belong" here on earth, he will conjure up in his mind various things he might be doing.

Another individual may not know how to respond to genuine love. He may feel that he is on the outside and that nobody cares. He may feel that he is a bother to people.

On the other hand, a person who has grown up in a happy home where emotional needs have been met will feel very differently. He is able to give and receive love. He doesn't feel that he has to control other people's lives. He can appreciate people who are not like him as well as those who are like him. He can have good relationships with people who are of the opposite sex without falling in love with them and becoming unduly attached to them. In other words, he can be close emotionally without becoming sexually or neurotically stirred.

A person whose emotional needs have been met in childhood feels that he is capable. He is willing to carry his share of the load. He is honest and truthful because he has no need to defend himself through various mechanisms. He has healthy feelings about himself. He does not fear people. He does not suspect that people are trying to "do him in." He respects people and trusts them easily. He can confront people in a kind way and not feel angry or embarrassed. In short, he is well adjusted, and God wants all His children to be well adjusted.

Solving these "inside problems" will enable people to live happier, healthier lives. Thus, they will be better able to live for the Lord and bring others, including their family members, to Him.

On the Alert for Child Sexual Abuse

"I wish they'd get child sex abuse out of the closet. People need to know that it takes place all the time." This statement was made by a woman who was telling about her own unhappy childhood experiences.

Today, sexual abuse of children is beginning to come out of the closet because as more and more children are being abused sexually, more people are willing to report it. Although incomplete, statistics are beginning to emerge. Many police officials express frustration because they can only guess the number of children actually being abused. In some police departments, extensive records are kept, but in others, few records are kept or sent to central offices. This problem is further aggravated by the fact that there are no comprehensive agencies to gather data, and not all victims are willing to report their experiences.

Police officials are certain of one thing, however. The problem appears to be increasing in all levels of society, not just in slums or poor housing districts. The dynamics that cause an adult to molest a child are at work in the minds of those who have good paying jobs as well as those who are unemployed. The problem may rear its ugly head in any community.

Children should be loved and protected, not victimized. It seems incredible that so many men (and some women) molest youngters, even infants. It seems unbelievable that between one-fifth and one-third of all women as children experienced some sort of sexual encounter with an adult male. Yet we must believe it. Certain conditions in society are setting the stage for increased child sexual abuse, and we must act to alter those conditions.

The Stage is Set

Stepfathers and live-in boy friends are often involved in child sexual abuse. A lack of commitment and love between such men and the child they are living with is often seen. As broken homes increase in number, more and more children will fall victim to those who do not really love them.

Marital discord and disturbed family relations are related to incestuous abuse. One study, for example, reported that 88 percent of the families studied were upset and disorganized before the incest occurred.

A substantial amount of research has shown an association between child sexual abuse and mothers being absent, sick, or alienated from their children. One report showed that

- Fifty-eight percent of a random survey of college girls who lived *without* their mothers some time before the age of sixteen had been sexually victimized—a rate three times that of the average girl in this group.
- Thirty-five percent of the girls whose mothers were often ill had been sexually victimized in childhood. This is a rate almost twice that of the average girl of the group.
- Thirty-eight percent of the girls whose mothers were not high school graduates were sexually victimized, twice the rate of the sample as a whole.

Incest is more likely to occur in families that are socially isolated. A man who has sexual intercourse with his daughter usually keeps her and the family away from activities in the community. Otherwise, people might discover it.

Confusion of roles within the family also causes homes to be more vulnerable. God has established roles for fathers, roles for mothers, and roles for children as delineated in chapters 5 and 6 of Ephesians. When the home functions as God ordained it, the benefits are multitudinous. When a family is upside down, it can never function properly. Girls with a working mother and an unemployed father, for example, are at a decided risk.

There is an association between alcohol and/or drug abuse and early incestuous experience. Forty-four percent of female drug abusers in one study and 70 percent of those in another reported having been sexually abused by a family member. Experts estimate that alcohol plays a role in over one-third of all reported cases of child sexual abuse.

There appears to be a relationship between mothers who were sexually abused in childhood by relatives and the incestuous abuse of their own little girls by their husbands. Fathers who were abused in their families while growing up, or who witnessed or participated in such abuse, are more likely to later sexually abuse their own children.

Today in the United States there is a one in four chance that a child will be the victim of incest, child molestation, or rape by the time he or she reaches eighteen. Incidence has increased alarmingly during the past fifteen years. The main reasons include:

1. The increased use of alcohol;
2. Increase in the number of stepfathers and live-in boy friends;
3. The larger number of daughters alone in the house with fathers, brothers, and uncles while mothers are out of the home;

4. The increased availability of pornography;
5. A gradual breakdown of established spiritual and moral values; and
6. Secularization of society.

Effects on the Victims

Are all people who are sexually abused damaged? Do all such children grow up to have significant problems? They usually do, depending upon various factors. Some modern "sex experts" disagree, but the convincing weight of overwhelming evidence proves otherwise.

Thousands of problem-laden people trace their ruined lives to childhood incestuous experiences. As children they were sexually abused time and time again. The effects are subtle, long-lasting, and devastating. Over 50 percent of the prostitutes queried in several studies reported a history of rape and incest.

It is important to use good judgment in dealing with a victimized child, but probably no amount of delicate handling will completely erase the terrible scars of repeated incest. The great harm comes *not* just in physical symptoms, but rather, in psychological damage.

Repeated molestation has serious effects on the victim. Its emotional and psychological impact is destructive, causing loss of self-esteem, intense feelings of guilt, and extreme tension. Many also suffer from intrusive thoughts, avoidance behavior, and gender identity conflicts. The conflicting emotions caused by such premature sexual experiences take a tremendous toll.

The following letter is typical of the ones I receive from women who have been violated as children, and it clearly illustrates how this woman's whole life was affected.

Dear Dr. Narramore:
  When I was a little girl I was with my uncle and he exposed

his body and made me do filthy sex acts. This was just one of many experiences. There were others. I never told anyone about these things. I was too scared. My mother always was at work. I feel she loved me but she didn't know what was happening to me while she was away at work—she still doesn't know.

I was a pretty child, but I didn't do well in school; I always got poor grades. I was not happy. I was insecure. I always ran with the wrong crowd. I couldn't make friends. I never felt I had anything to offer them. At the age of 16 I became pregnant and got married. I am still married, and we have three beautiful children.

My husband and I were married about one and a half years when we were saved. Now we both love the Lord very much. I have told my husband some of the things about my past but I don't think he really understands me. He loves me and is good to me. I love him, but down deep I felt all I've been good for is sex. I can't really trust him or receive his love as I should.

I have hidden these things for so long I sometimes don't know what to do. My mother never explained to me. I thought sex was dirty. I was introduced to such sinful things at such a young age.

If you know any way to help me please let me know. I listen almost every day to you on the radio and appreciate you very much.

Misconceptions about Pedophiles

Who sexually abuses children? What are these people like? An intensive study of 148 such offenders in Massachusetts revealed some surprising facts that run counter to common assumptions. The following *misconceptions* are some they listed.

The child offender is a dirty old man. Actually only 1 percent of the subjects in this study were over age fifty-five. More than 80 percent of the men were under thirty years of age when they committed their first known pedophiliac offense.

The offender is a stranger to his victim. Almost three-fourths of the victims were well acquainted with those who violated their sexual privacy. Parents often attempt to protect their youngsters by advising them not to talk to strangers. That's good advice, but it doesn't appear to offer much protection from child molesters. The sex abuser is likely to be living in the home! It is likely to be the child's father, stepfather, uncle, brother, or grandfather.

The child molester is retarded. In this study all the subjects were carefully checked. There was no significant difference between their levels of intelligence and that of the general population. They were no more likely to be retarded than anyone else.

The child offender is alcoholic or drug addicted. This study indicated that although some were intoxicated when their assaults took place, and some of the offenders blamed their problem on alcohol, there was not always a direct connection.

The child offender is a sexually frustrated person. It is sometimes claimed that sex abusers turn to children because their sexual needs are not being met otherwise. The fact that much father-daughter incest takes place when the mother is either ill or absent from the home appears to add some credence to this supposition. But those who conducted this study were not convinced that the offender is sexually frustrated.

The child molester is insane. The demented "sex fiend" is a frightening stereotype. Fortunately, such cases appear to be rare exceptions. Only 5 percent of the subjects showed clinical evidence of psychosis.

Child offenders progress over time to increasingly violent acts. The assumption that the offender will repeat is a legitimate one. But his type of crime may not change appreciably.

Characteristics of Pedophiles

Now let's look at some of the specific characteristics that may be common to pedophiles. Virtually all pedophiles have low self-images. In nearly every instance, their childhoods were unhappy and unfulfilled. Their basic emotional needs were not met adequately by their parents. Day by day they experienced negative treatment. They become emotionally deprived. The experiences that should have gone into their lives to make them feel happy and healthy about themselves escaped them. By the time they reach adulthood, they feel sorely inadequate. They feel that they do not measure up to other people. Down deep they harbor feelings that cause them to turn away from adult sexual contacts. Instead, they turn toward young children who do not make them feel inadequate or inferior.

As a boy is growing up normally, he has many daily experiences which make him feel adequate and which develop his healthy self-esteem. These experiences are with his parents, siblings, teachers, other children, and adults in general. Day by day and year by year he feels good about himself and about the opposite sex. He thinks of girls as desirable. He is not threatened by them; rather, he feels adequately masculine in their presence.

In time he becomes interested in dating. Eventually he falls in love and gets married. Sexual intercourse with his wife is normal and delightful. He feels adequate and comfortable in their relationship. This is normal psychosexual development.

With the pedophile, these experiences never took place, and as an adult, he feels incapable and threatened by sexual intercourse with a wife. That is too overwhelming, too demanding, too frightening. Yet he has sex drives which crave relief. So he turns away from adult women and to little children, sometimes boys, sometimes girls, depending upon his personality dynamics.

Rarely does he understand the experiences that have turned him to his unnatural path. And merely knowing it would not automatically change him. The problem is much deeper and persistent than that.

People often ask, "Don't pedophiles give any thought to the welfare of the child they are abusing? Don't they understand that it's going to injure them? Some of them are businessmen and leaders of youth. Aren't they smart enough to know that what they're doing to a child is a terrible, harmful thing that will haunt him for years?" Frankly, the pedophile's thinking doesn't lie in such directions. He is driven by what he wants. He is intent upon his own desires and meeting them through a young child. Furthermore he justifies what he is doing, and in time he believes his justification. He doesn't have to think twice about the right or wrong. He goes ahead and does it.

Sixty-eight children are molested on the average by each pedophile, according to Dr. Gene G. Abel, director of the Sexual Behavior Clinic at the New York State Psychiatric Institution.

Are pedophiles homosexual or heterosexual? Do they prefer sex with little boys or with young girls? Actually, their sexual preference depends upon the specific dynamics and experiences of the years they were growing up. Some pedophiles prefer boys, others prefer girls.

Can Pedophiles Change?

The most likely way by which a pedophile may experience change is through intense, long-term professional psychological counseling along with a saving faith in the Lord Jesus Christ. When such a person becomes a Christian, he has different attitudes: "Old things have passed away; behold, all things have become new" (2 Cor. 5:17). But the person must want help; he must want to change.

Obviously, a person does not need to be a believer in Jesus Christ in order *not* to be a pedophile. Millions of people are not Christians, yet they surely are *not* abusers of children. Consequently, it would be incorrect to say that a person had to be a born-again Christian in order to avoid being a pedophile. Pedophiliac tendencies are not necessarily caused by being unsaved. The problem is not necessarily a spiritual one. There are other causes, as we have seen.

However, being saved gives a person a new nature. It gives him new power and new desires. It brings control and godliness into his life. God's Holy Spirit who indwells the believer cleanses his life and gives him fulfillment and joy. In other words, no matter what problem an individual may have, being saved helps him. In fact, it is the most powerful dynamic that can come into a person's life. Many men who have abused children have given their hearts to Christ, and in time they have grown into godly men who hated even the thought of sexual abuse.

A study of pedophiles would show that they have many disturbances and problems. They are always characterized by psychological hang-ups and deviations. They have problems "all over." Therefore, when a person who abuses children sexually resolves his deep psychological problems through professional counseling, he is likely to lose his desire to abuse children. However, researchers are quick to point out that most pedophiles do not respond well to typical counseling. Few seem to be helped.

Why is it difficult to change and rehabilitate a pedophile? Why doesn't he respond to instruction, punishment, or public disdain? The basic reason can be found in his attitudes and behavior which are quite solidly crystallized. You might think of them as cement which once was wet and soft and pliable, but which has set a long time and now is resistant to impressions of most any kind.

The pedophile's feelings and attitudes have been developing day by day, month by month, and year by year since early infancy. Now he acts and responds in a rather consistent, predictable manner, and change is difficult.

Child sex abusers are sometimes employed in jobs such as school teachers, recreation specialists, camp supervisors, and other child-related occupations. Of course, the majority of men and women who are engaged in such work are normal, and they respect the children and enjoy the work. But wise parents will follow the example of one mother who confided, "I was delighted when my son finally got a man teacher. But I listen closely when my boy talks about what goes on in his classroom." So should all parents.

Just who should you trust with your children? That can be a difficult problem. For example, a seventy-six-year-old grandmother owned a reputable, well-established preschool in California. In 1984 she was charged with a long series of sex crimes against some of her pupils. Accused along with her were her daughter, son-in-law, grandson, granddaughter, and a fifty-six-year-old woman who formerly taught at the school. According to newspaper reports, pupils are believed to have been subjected to all kinds of sexual perversions. Parents in the community were astonished. These child caretakers didn't appear to be the kind of people who would engage in such depraved activity.

The sad truth is, it's not always easy to tell. Many wonder why such perverted individuals are not rounded up, given therapy, and cured. The process just isn't that simple. It's difficult to apprehend and convict such people. The criminal justice system must carefully guard against crank complaints. After all, a family may be almost ruined if an innocent person is unjustly convicted. After a culprit is caught, psychotherapy seldom benefits him unless he wants to change. And that is usually not the case.

Incest

Incest involves sexual relations between family members or close realtives. Perhaps the most common forms of incest are sexual relations between brothers and sisters, between fathers and daughters, between stepfathers and stepdaughters, between uncles and nieces, and between grandfathers and granddaughters.

Although incestuous relationships can exist between grownups who are close relatives, we will direct our attention toward adults who force sexual relations upon children and teen-agers. No one knows the frequency of such crimes. Estimates range from one million to ten million cases a year. In Los Angeles County alone, reports of incest increased from 420 to 2,285 over a period of less than ten years. Regardless of the numerical facts, we know that it is a serious problem that plagues families in every country around the world.

A Case History

One of my close personal friends is Dr. Maurice E. Wagner, a mature Christian psychologist who has a large counseling practice. Recently I interviewed him, calling upon his extensive experience as a therapist. The following conversation will undoubtedly yield some helpful insights into this problem.

NARRAMORE: Why should a man sexually abuse a child? What goes on in his mind?

WAGNER: I've observed that in any kind of sexual dysfunction, people tend to relate sexually at the level they have developed psychosexually. They may be adult physically but childlike psychosexually.

NARRAMORE: What do you mean by *psychosexual*?

WAGNER: *Psychosexual* pertains to a person's thinking and feeling about his sexuality. A person relates sexually in terms of his own commitment and involvement with the other person.

Take, for example, a man who has had sexual intercourse with three of his little daughters. His wife divorced him, so he began dating another woman. Then he had the gall to molest his girl friend's daughters.

Because of his parents' attitudes, this man had no opportunity in childhood to accept himself as a male. He got his own way at home by remaining like a child. Certain types of domination were taking place in the home by immature parents. Consequently, he remained like a child psychosexually. So when he became a husband, his sexual behavior with his wife was immature.

When his children began to grow, he would get them away from their mother and play with them. He needed sexual gratification without any personal involvement or responsibility. As long as the child didn't protest, he felt he was getting by with it.

NARRAMORE: When he did this with his little daughters, did they come to blame themselves, thinking they were causing it?

WAGNER: I am sure they must have. They usually do. I didn't get acquainted with the daughters, but from what I understand, one daughter when grown became frigid; another daughter became totally promiscuous with no conscience about sex. The third daughter is trying to make a go of her marriage.

By the way, the man did not feel he had done his daughters an injustice. He had no real guilt.

NARRAMORE: Why?

WAGNER: He didn't have any real guilt because he viewed sex like a little boy...being curious about what the organs looked like, what they felt like. He was more or less interacting on the level of "let's play and see what things are like," instead of having a mature, personal involvement.

NARRAMORE: Did he not see that this would cause them to have serious problems for the rest of their lives?

WAGNER: He didn't have enough character development to take responsibility for it by saying, "I have harmed my daughters." He could say the words if he thought that would get him leniency.

NARRAMORE: Did the sisters know that he was molesting the others?

WAGNER: Sometimes he had relations with all three at once. But he maintained strict secrecy through threats and through self-pity and bribes. The mother was working out of the home. He approached the daughters slowly, and made it pleasant enough so they would not feel pain or discomfort. To a point they would finally enjoy sex with him. As a result, he took pride in being a successful lover, and he had no particular guilt about it.

NARRAMORE: If he had no guilt, why did he seek professional help?

WAGNER: He was seeking professional help because his girl friend discovered it and turned him in. In fact, he would have no problem at all getting up in church and waving his arms to lead the choir.

NARRAMORE: You're saying that a pedophile might go for years doing these things without feeling guilty about them?

WAGNER: I've seldom seen a pedophile who had any real repentant guilt.

NARRAMORE: Is a pedophile difficult to work with in therapy? Does he respond favorably?

WAGNER: My experience is this: I have not found enough character in that type of man—enough maturity in his psychosexual development—to have strong guilt feelings about anything sexual.

NARRAMORE: So he would not respond to treatment?

WAGNER: The only treatment he would respond to would be conditioned reflex: "If I touch another child, I will get jailed. I'll lose my liberties."

NARRAMORE: Do you think in some cases it would be possible to help a pedophile? A Christian therapist has so much spiritually going for him—he knows the Lord, he knows the Word of God. He has a whole spiritual arsenal to bring to play. Would it be possible for a pedophile to develop guilt feelings so the counselor would be able to help him?

WAGNER: I would assume it might take at least five years of intensive therapy, because this man needs almost total reparenting. He would have to make a sufficiently close bond to the therapist in order to work through much of his psychosexual development. I've gone this way with a few people—not only pedophiles, but with others who need reparenting. And it takes a long time to get them through the various levels of normal child development. A pedophile may not have any real conviction about his behavior. He is so anxious to get the world to accept him. His insecurity is soothed by playing up to people and being almost sociopathic in the sense that he wants everybody to like him, therefore, he does not take responsibility for his own misconduct.

Incest is especially harmful because it's committed by a family member who, of all people, should be especially kind and respectful to a child. But instead, the father, stepfather, uncle, grandfather, or brother is taking advantage of the child. If respect and wholesome affection is not forthcoming from a relative, then where is it coming from? Usually no place and no one. When a young girl has been betrayed by a family member she trusts, she usually develops severe psychological problems that remain for the rest of her life.

Spiritual Implications

Another insidious problem develops that is spiritual in nature. Briefly stated, it's this: Great spiritual truths are correlated with and understood through the family institution. The Bible clearly teaches that God is our heavenly Father. A little girl, for example, comes to understand that God is much like her earthly father, stepfather, uncle, or grandfather. But if this earthly example is an incest perpetrator, the child will be seriously confused about what God is like.

God also teaches in His eternal Word that if we become converted—admitting and forsaking our sins and accepting Christ as our personal Savior—we become the children of God. Here again, we see another beautiful relationship in which we can depend upon God our heavenly Father (like our earthly father) to love His children, care and provide for them, and keep them from harm. But if this example has been incestuous, the child may come to hate and distrust God, too.

Another great spiritual correlation is that every human being who trusts in Christ as his personal Savior is related to every other true believer. In short, we should love, honor, and respect our earthly brothers and sisters and stepbrothers and stepsisters. Again if this relationship has been a negative one, the child's mind may fill with distrust and suspicion.

As we read the Word we learn that we born-again Christians constitute the unblemished bride of Christ. We are the blood-bought ones who are without spot or stain. But if a family member who is a churchgoer and supposedly a Christian has betrayed a child by raping her, the child's concept of Christians can be extremely distorted. Such a child can grow up to dislike everything pertaining to Christianity.

Can you imagine the inner turmoil caused by a child's imagining the heavenly Father to be like the father or grandfather who has violated and seduced her? Or the effects of years of sordid memories on her as a young adult?

Can you imagine the confusion and hatred that boils within a person as he is told in the Word of God and as he hears from the pulpit, that he is the beloved child of a heavenly Father?

Can you imagine the distorted feelings and attitudes a girl may develop when she thinks of her spiritual brothers and sisters around the world in light of the brother who forced her to have sex with him?

When God sent His Son Jesus Christ into the world, He could have introduced Him as a grown man ready to do the will of God. But he didn't. God brought His Son Jesus Christ into a humble family. God established the family not only to continue the human race and to honor Him, but also to make it easy for us to understand the nature of God, to understand our relationship to God, and to know our responsibility to Him. Volumes could be written about how we can understand God and His plan for mankind through loving, respectful relationships in a family. But this is essentially destroyed and perverted through an incestuous relationship.

After this rather intensive look at this disturbing crime against children, I hope you will come away with several points uppermost in your minds. (1) Child sexual abuse is common. (2) Parents and other adults should be alert to possible abuses of the children entrusted to them. (3) Families, schools, and other organizations that care for children should carefully screen employees who work closely with children. (4) Parents should make every effort to help their children to grow up in healthy ways so that they will not become abusive adults. (5) Professional counselors and law enforcement agencies should seek better ways to rehabilitate sex abusers. (6) Every effort should be made to help those innocent boys and girls who have been abused.

Childhood should be a relatively carefree time in which children are protected and reassured by parents and other adults. Memories of childhood should be of pleasant experiences, not of sordid, shame-filled ones. How bright a child's future will be if he has a happy, healthy Christian home life and parents he can trust!

CHAPTER

11

God Is Pleased

The day usually begins rather early at the Narramore home in Southern California. People on the East Coast start phoning about their problems at eight o'clock their time (five o'clock California time). A man may call and say, "Dr. Narramore, my pastor has suggested I call you. My wife is very depressed and we don't know where to go to get help. Can you give us the name of a Christian psychologist or someone who can help her?"

I always encourage callers as they seek professional help. I believe God is pleased when we use His system for getting well. God has given each person certain talents and interests, and as we develop these gifts, He enables us to help others. For example, both a dentist and an attorney have special talents and training. The nature of our immediate problem determines which one we need at the time. Just because both are talented doesn't mean we need only one of them. We need them both, and they need each other.

A year or so ago my wife, Ruth, and I were riding along the freeway one morning on our way to the office. Preparing to pass a car, I stepped on the accelerator, but the car didn't respond. In fact, it slowed down. Perplexed, I stepped on it again, but the car went even slower. Just then I began to think about the emergency phones along the highway. Little by little I changed lanes and got over into the right lane, praying that my car would roll to a stop right by one of those emergency phones. Sure enough, it did.

"What's wrong?" Ruth asked.

"I don't know, I'll have to take a look." I said, with a measure of false confidence.

If I had been smart, or better still, if I hadn't been a typical egotistical male, I would have gotten out of the car, stepped over to the phone, and immediately called a tow truck to take us to a nearby garage.

But, I wanted to impress my wife. So I lifted up the hood and fiddled around for a moment with several of those mechanical gadgets. Naturally there were hundreds of them!

Then I said, "Okay, Ruth, turn on the ignition." Ruth did, but of course, nothing happened.

"It still doesn't start," she said.

Then to protect my male ego, I explained that these new cars are very complex. I looked under the hood again, and I poked a number of gadgets. Then I said to my wife, "Now, honey, will you try the ignition again?"

Ruth turned the key again, but still nothing happened. Then she stuck her head out the window and said, "Do you know what I think?"

"No, what do you think?" I replied.

"I don't think you know anything about what you're doing!" she said.

And of course she was right. I wasn't a mechanic and I knew it. But I wanted her to think that I understood such things and that I was on top of every situation. I should have called for the tow truck in the first place!

So I pushed the hood down, stepped over to the phone, and called for help. A few minutes later the truck arrived and towed us to a nearby garage.

Immediately the mechanic came out and asked what our problem was. He took a look under the hood, went back inside the garage, and brought out a little gadget. He took the old one off, put on the new one, and said, "Now turn your key."

I did, and the car started immediately.

Is it too much to say that my seeking help from another person pleased God? That's His system here on earth to help people. Each of us uses his talents and interests. We develop skills, then we serve others. When we need their help, they serve us. Too many people, including Christians, hesitate to use God's method for resolving their problems. For years, they chug along on about three cylinders, when they could have gotten help and functioned on all eight!

God has given many Christian people the ability to counsel and help resolve problems, and He is pleased when we use their services. Yet there are obstacles that keep people from getting professional help. One is that people simply don't know *when* they need help. Another is that a series of roadblocks steer people away from seeking the help they need. Let's take a closer look at these roadblocks—or excuses.

Twelve Roadblocks to Professional Help

1. "Which way do I go?" Somehow people know how to go to restaurants, to school, to church, to department stores and other places, but when it comes to obtaining professional help for their emotional problems, they don't know how to go about it. As a result, many of them don't get any help at all. Special help is available from several sources.

Family physicians. Oftentimes doctors are familiar with specialists in various fields. A physician who knows your family's record and history may be able to give proper referral.

Medical agencies. Questions about professional counseling are fairly common to the operators at the switchboard of a medical facility, such as a hospital or clinic. They often have a list of area counselors that you may contact.

Local church. Especially if the church is large, the church secretary may get several calls a day asking about counseling. She is often able to recommend fine, Christian professionals.

The Narramore Christian Foundation. Through the years, we have developed a list of Christian psychologists and psychiatrists throughout the United States and, in some cases, other countries.

2. "What will it cost?" I suppose nearly everyone has heard stories about someone paying large sums of money to get help, but it isn't always that expensive. Many people are able to obtain professional help free or at a nominal cost in their community. True, any kind of professional help is expensive. Having your teeth worked on costs plenty. Getting your car repaired costs money. *But it is cheaper in the long run to get help now than to let things go.* This is true of material possessions. How much more important it is for you to receive help for your emotional problems that affect your entire outlook on life.

3. "I guess I'll adjust." In many cases people adjust, to some degree, to their problems. It's sort of like having a hitching post in the middle of your living room. Many people would take it out, but others would just work around it. Somehow they would get along with a post—and a couple of horses—in the middle of their living room! And so it is with problems, especially marriage problems. For example, "Mr. Jones" is a very passive person. He's married to a woman who is very aggressive and domineering. Early in their marriage, the husband learned to "zip his lip." He saw that the best way *not* to have quarrels was to be quiet. True, he was boiling on the inside, so it was bothering him in physical ways and he had various physical symptoms. This couple lived together for fifty years in this way—she dominating, he

remaining quiet. They became partially adjusted to their problem and lived a rather "happy/miserable" Christian life.

4. "It would be so embarrassing." Some people have a rather low concept of themselves and do not want to admit to themselves, much less to others, that they have a problem. They keep it buried the best they can, though it may be obvious to the people around them that there may be a problem. But the individual never makes a move to get professional help because of potential embarrassment.

5. "What would people think?" Some people are leaders in their community, job, or church, and the last thing they want anyone to know is that they haven't been able to manage their own lives. I know a minister, who has a very serious emotional problem, but he keeps hiding it. He doesn't want anyone in the congregation or community to know. Of course, he doesn't stand alone. Millions of people are like him. They are more concerned about what the community would think than about their futures, so they avoid seeking professional help and continue suffering.

6. "What can they do for me anyway?" Many people have resigned themselves to their lives as they are. Somehow their attitude becomes one of bearing a cross. "Everyone is carrying *some* kind of load," they say, so they'll carry one too. They can't imagine being well. They doubt there is help for them from any source.

7. "My family says no." Some people are prevented from obtaining help because a family member opposes it. A wife wants to get help, but her husband is against it.

Occasionally, the reverse is true. The husband tries to persuade his wife to get professional help, but she refuses it because some other member of the family—perhaps her mother—doesn't want her to get such help. On a number of occasions teen-agers have called the counseling center at the

Narramore Christian Foundation and have asked, "If I come, will you tell my parents?" They have explained that their parents were very much opposed to their seeking help. If these young people are to get help for their problems, they will have to sneak away to do it. Indeed, one's own household may be his worst enemy.

8. "Just trust and obey." Some people feel that the Lord will work it out somehow if they are just more spiritual. These people feel that if they read a few more verses in the Bible, pray more and longer, or do something of a spiritual nature, God will work it out. Actually, God usually uses human beings to help other human beings. That's His plan on earth.

True, there is no other way but to trust and obey, but God often wants us to trust and obey by listening to His servants. A good example of this is found in 2 Kings. A Syrian captain was told to go to Elisha, the prophet, who would heal him of leprosy. When the captain sought out Elisha, he was told to wash in the Jordan River seven times to be healed (see 2 Kings 5:10). That's not exactly the cure the captain had expected, but it worked! God may be asking you to trust and obey by seeking a Christian psychologist and benefitting from his or her expertise.

9. "I tried it and it didn't work." Not long ago I was talking with a woman who said she had already had some sessions with a psychologist. I asked her what happened. "Nothing," she said. I further inquired, "Have you ever thought that perhaps someone else could help you?" She said she hadn't thought of that. I then asked if the therapist she had gone to was a Christian. "No," she replied. That was probably part of the answer to her dissatisfaction right there. Simply because you have seen a professional counselor and that person has not helped you doesn't mean that no one can help you. Some stores may not sell the particular

item you want to buy, but other stores do! It may be necessary for you to seek out another counselor.

10. "What about religious tampering?" Many believers are concerned that the counselor may not be a Christian and that he would give unscriptural advice. It is true that many psychiatrists and psychologists do not know Christ as their Savior, and their counsel is far from sound and biblical. As a result some patients have been hurt rather than helped. But increasingly, there are highly trained, skilled psychologists, both men and women, who love the Lord. And they will not make fun of a person's stand on the Word of God. Nevertheless, fear of having their faith questioned or attacked does keep many people from seeking professional help.

11. "Why didn't someone tell me sooner?" Through the years I've been amazed to talk to so many people who became very surprised when I told them that there was help for people with problems like theirs. They replied that they didn't know anything could be done for their type of problem. They had grown accustomed to it and had supposed they were doomed to live with it.

12. "Time will take care of it." Some people are simply waiting and hoping that things will improve. They feel that if another week, another month, or another year goes by, things will get a little better. But that is seldom the case. Usually, their emotional problems mount. Just waiting or hoping that things will change doesn't solve problems. They need attention—expert attention.

Warning! Professional Help Needed

People often ask me if I think their problem is serious enough for them to seek professional help. Not long ago a couple talked to me about their daughter. They were not sure if she should seek professional help. As they talked I could tell that their daughter did have a very serious problem. Actually, she should have had help years before, but they had just waited. If they had been able to recognize some warning signals in her behavior, she could have received help much sooner.

How can you tell if your situation is serious enough to call for assistance from a specialist? I believe there are at least eight recognizable signs that indicate professional help is needed.

1. *General unhappiness.* Life is basically a happy experience. Of course, unhappiness and sorrow slip into every life from time to time, and this can be expected. God has not promised blue skies forever. However, life for the most part is happy. When a person is *chronically unhappy* over a period of time, it usually means that he is far from enjoying good emotional and mental health. No one need go through life unhappy. The solution so often lies in seeking the right professional help.

2. *Vocational problems.* If in your daily work you are continually unhappy or not doing a good job, you should do something about it. Many people spend their days at a job they thoroughly dislike or one that affects their well-being. If you are having trouble on the job, you should seek professional help.

3. *Aches and pains.* Many times your body will tell you when you need help. The turmoil in your life may be so great that you are continually having backaches and/or headaches. Because God has made us three-part beings, many times *emotional* disturbances and *spiritual* problems show themselves in *physical* ways. Not long ago I was talking with a woman who had a terrible burning sensation at the end of her fingers which would recur several times a day. Since there didn't seem to be any recognizable cause, I suggested that she get professional help. After she had a number

of sessions with a psychologist, the pain disappeared. In her case the pain was an indication and symptom of emotional distress and that she needed help.

4. *Spiritual ineffectiveness and immaturity.* To the Christian, prayer should be a joy. Bible reading should be a pleasant, heartwarming experience. A Christian should find real satisfaction in sharing his faith with others, but many people do not experience this joy. They feel that their prayers don't reach the ceiling. To such persons Bible reading is a chore. And witnessing? They would be frightened to death to try it. If you have these kinds of problems, perhaps you should talk to your pastor or some other counselor so that you can get going for God.

5. *Difficult to live with.* Many people are difficult to live and work with. They cause everyone around them to suffer. Jane is always screaming at her children, and her children can't stand it. (A teen-age girl once told me that she wished her mother would drop dead. "She's yelling and screaming at us all the time.") Naturally this mother needs help. When a person's daily experience is not fulfilling or gratifying, the person may become difficult to live with. But there *is* help, and this person should take steps to avail herself or himself of it.

6. *Poor school work.* Many children do well in school, but others do not. When a child is having problems with school work and all efforts to aid him fail, he needs professional help.

I had the joy of serving as a psychologist on the staff of the Los Angeles County Superintendent of Schools. During that time, I went to various school districts and consulted with teachers regarding students who were doing poor school work. In nearly every case, I was able to help them to resolve their problems and do better work in school. Specialized help is available for these students.

7. *Unable to cope daily.* Many people cannot face living. You may have heard the expression, "Stop the world; I want to get off." This is another way of saying that one cannot cope with what is going on day by day. Too much is pressing in on him. The tensions are too great. When a person is unable to cope with his daily living, he need not settle for this kind of day-by-day frustration. He can obtain help.

8. *Exaggerated and inappropriate emotional responses.* One way to determine if a person needs help is to consider his emotional responses. There is nothing wrong with daydreaming, if it is done in moderation. When someone daydreams nearly all the time, he may need professional help.

Another person is extremely depressed most of the time. This is a sure sign of the need for professional help. Oh, we all experience little bouts of depression, but we know it's temporary and we can handle it. The "always" depressed person should seek help.

The person who cries a great deal, seemingly for any or for no reason, is not exhibiting normal behavior. The person does need professional help.

Once I counseled with a man who had temper tantrums. If his behavior had been occasional, it would not be too unusual, because everybody loses his temper at times. This man blew his top many times a day and was like a little child. It was evident to me that this man had a mild neurological impairment (brain damage), but he didn't know it. He needed professional help.

Why Isn't the Bible Enough?

Sometimes people raise the question, "Why is it not enough just to rely on the Scriptures to keep us on an even balance and able to cope with life?" For a great majority of people this is enough. But since Christians are also physical

GOD IS PLEASED

beings and emotional beings, some problems are in those specific areas. So God uses physicians, counselors, and other trained professionals.

I know of a woman who for years, whenever opportunity was given for a testimony, invariably quoted the verse, "God has not given us a spirit of fear, but of power and of love and of a sound mind" (2 Tim. 1:7). An insightful pastor might have questioned why this Christian woman continually reiterated this verse. He might have questioned whether she was not, in fact, trying to reassure herself. It was a sad time for that pastor and for the whole church when this devout woman, a genuine soul winner, began to withdraw from people, to act strangely, unpredictably, and completely out of character. She finally isolated herself in her room, refusing to see even close friends with whom she had spent hours in prayer throughout the years. Obviously she needed professional help. Many people suffer and are misunderstood because their problem is not recognized for what it is: a psychological disturbance whose cause can be determined and for which treatment is available.

Remember, it is important to

- know that definite, recognizable signs indicate the need for professional help;
- determine that it's time the person obtain professional help on the basis of these symptoms;
- understand that it is a good, common-sense thing for one to admit he has a problem and to seek solutions;
- ask, "What is preventing me from getting the help I need?"; and
- realize that Christ-centered help may be more available than you think and find where to go.

Our burdens can be lifted if we will admit to our problems

169

and seek out help to solve those problems. No one has to be stuck in a valley of despair. When we use God's system to get well, He is pleased, and when we are well and whole, we are able to live more fully for Him. We cannot do less for Him.

Where to Turn

The Taylors were shocked when they answered the knock at the door and saw their neighbor, Helen, leaning against the wall, sobbing. Her eyes had already started to blacken and her jaw had swollen. The blood on her chin and blouse had started to dry.

"He's so angry," Helen said as she struggled to separate herself from the wall. "He's never hit me so hard before. Can you help me?"

The Taylors knew Helen's husband had a hot temper, but they never knew that he beat her. As they helped her inside their house, she began telling the horrors of this and past beatings. It became clear that something had to be done.

Legal action was the obvious step, but Helen didn't want to call the police. She just wanted to get out of the house, stay somewhere until she could pull herself together, and decide what steps to take. But where could she go?

Unfortunately, there are not enough answers to this question.

When police come to homes like Helen's, they usually suggest that the wife and children leave the house, not the husband. Even when a husband is arrested, the wife doesn't feel safe in the house because she knows he'll be back as soon as he can.

Sometimes family, neighbors, or friends may take the victim in. But often this is not possible. So where does a battered, abused wife or child go?

The Care of Victims

There are not enough shelters for victims of abuse. One reason is because so little has been known about the problem. Only recently have records been kept, laws enacted, widespread public interest shown. As a result, the facilities available are usually of recent origin.

Another reason is because of the expense involved. It costs a great deal to house, feed, clothe, and care for mothers or children. Nearly two million children a year are victims of parental abuse and neglect. Nearly six million wives are abused annually. There are four thousand reported cases of sexual abuse every year in New York alone, and this figure doesn't include all the other categories of abused people. The existing facilities are insufficient to handle so many people. Providing the needed services for such a large number of abuse victims is more than many communities feel capable of assuming.

What Is Needed

Karen was working hard to support her family. Her husband, Frank, had been unemployed for over a year, and Karen was the sole breadwinner. She never suspected that she could be a battered wife, but Frank's frustrations had reached their peak. He could no longer control himself, and before either knew it, Frank had struck Karen hard enough to require a trip to the hospital emergency ward.

Two types of programs are needed to help situations like Karen's and Frank's. First, Karen needs a place where she can live in safety until it is possible for her to return to a peaceful home. The shelter may have to accommodate children as well. These homes must provide beds, food, clothes, and medical care—all without cost—to the victims. Some women may have jobs, but many who would come to these shelters have no income. In some cases, these shelters may provide training and education for the women, so they will be able to support themselves and, if necessary, start a new life. Also, there is a need for day care for children of battered women who are involved in court action. (Although there are homes for battered children and some facilities for battered women, virtually no services are available for battered men.)

Second, rehabilitation programs are needed for abusers. In Frank's case, he needs not only a job but also counseling to help him understand and deal with his anger and frustration.

Battered wives and abusive husbands are not the only ones in need of places to turn. Abused and neglected children also need help. Fortunately, they are usually more satisfactorily cared for than other abused individuals. Some hospitals and other medical facilities have an institution for emergency and short-term care. More of these places are needed. For longer terms of shelter, foster homes are available.

Some churches, foundations, cities, counties, states, and other organizations have established homes or a network of homes for children. Boys and girls are placed in large family-style environments and are free to attend school and live normal lives with those who have come from similar backgrounds. Unfortunately, these homes, especially those sponsored by churches and Christian organizations, are few. As a result, little spiritual emphasis is available to most victims.

Helping the children is only part of the answer. The parents who abuse children need help. Most of the abused children are eventually returned to their parents. Half of the severely abused children who return home eventually die at their parents' hands. Simply separating the parent and child for a time does not teach a parent not to abuse.

Care for the elderly is available for those who can afford to pay, but desirable services for nonaffluent people are not easy to come by. The same is true for the handicapped in need of special attention or education. Some large cities have good programs for the disabled or mentally retarded, but in smaller communities, many of these people are left alone in homes during the day.

What Is Available

Although the demand for more help organizations and shelters is great, some facilities and organizations are already established and ready to help. The following organizations provide specialized services for troubled families. This list is by no means complete, because the picture is continually changing, but it is a source from which to receive wider information.

Salvation Army. Such services as temporary foster home care for children, prenatal and postnatal counseling, care and guidance for unwed and expectant mothers, and counseling for unmarried fathers are offered.

Parents Anonymous. Parents Anonymous is a self-help group for parents under stress with more than fifteen hundred groups throughout the United States. There are no costs, and no one is required to reveal his real name. Group members support and encourage one another in searching out positive alternatives to the abusive behavior in their lives. You may locate the Parents Anonymous in your area by calling the toll-free-hotline number, 800-421-0353 (in California, call 800-352-0386).

National Committee for the Prevention of Child Abuse. Write to 332 South Michigan Avenue, Chicago, Illinois 60604.

Big Brothers/Big Sisters of America. Volunteers work with children in need of friendship and guidance under the direction of a professionally trained staff. Special emphasis is placed on families under stress and single-parent homes. The national office is located at 117 S. 17th Street, Suite 1200, Philadelphia, Pennsylvania 19103. 215-567-2748. Call the national office or a local agency listed in your telephone directory.

National Clearinghouse for Mental Health Information. Services available include inpatient and outpatient care, emergency twenty-four-hour care, consultation and education, comprehensive programs for children and the elderly, court screening, aftercare programs, halfway house programs, treatment of alcoholism and drug abuse. 5600 Fishers Lane, Rockville, Maryland 20857. 301-443-4515. (Note: These services are at various locations throughout the U.S.)

Juvenile Assistance of McClean, Ltd. Family Growth Center. Free counseling is provided to families who are troubled by abuse. There are special discussion groups for adolescents. P.O. Box 637, McLean, Virginia 22101. 703-356-2045.

National Runaway Switchboard. A national hotline designed to help runaway children and their parents. Referrals are made to children without shelter. The toll-free hotline number outside Illinois is 800-621-4000; in Illinois it is 800-972-6004.

Huckleberry House, Inc. Counseling is provided to disturbed teen-agers and their families. They also provide some housing for runaways. 1421 Hamlet Street, Columbus, Ohio 43201. 614-294-5553.

Military Family Resource Center. This international center supports family advocacy in the military services. It also provides technical assistance to professionals who serve military families. 6501 Loisdale Ct., Suite 900, Springfield, Virginia 22150. 703-922-7671.

National Coalition Against Domestic Violence. This national membership organization is composed of independently operated shelters for battered women and their families. 1728 N. Street, NW, Washington, D.C. 20036. 202-347-7015.

Formerly Abused Children Emerging in Society (FACES). A self-help group set up for adults who were abused as children and are experiencing difficulty in coping as a result of the abuse. It also provides technical assistance on setting up local chapters. 71 Haynes Street, Manchester, Connecticut 06040. 203-646-1222.

Parents Without Partners, Inc. Activities and mutual help groups are provided for single parents and their children in all fifty states, Canada, and Europe. 7910 Woodmont Avenue, Bethesda, Maryland 20814. 301-654-8850.

Single Dad's Lifestyle. A twenty-four-hour hotline helps dads locate resources nationwide. It publishes the "Single Dad's Lifestyle Blue List of Father's Rights and Divorce Reform Organizations," and copies will be sent free to anyone sending a self-addressed, stamped envelope. P.O. Box 4842, Scottsdale, Arizona 85258. 602-998-0980.

American Humane Association, Children's Division. Program planning, consultation, and education and training are offered to individuals and communities creating child protective services. 9725 E. Hampden, Denver, Colorado 80231. 303-695-0811.

National Center on Child Abuse and Neglect, Children's Bureau. This agency administers federal HHS funds for prevention and treatment of child abuse, research, and demonstration projects. P.O. Box 1182, Washington, D.C. 20013. 202-245-2840.

Children's Defense Fund. The fund deals with the education, care, welfare, and health of children, and with advocacy affecting legislation in these areas. A telephone service is available for those wanting current information. A newsletter is available on a subscription basis. 1520 New Hampshire Avenue, NW, Washington, D.C. 20036. 800-424-9602.

Child Welfare League of America. Care and services for deprived, neglected, and dependent children and their families are provided. 67 Irving Place, New York, New York 10003. 212-254-7410.

New organizations are developing all the time. The names and phone numbers of helping organizations in your community are usually available by calling your local law enforcement department. Information may also be available from some churches.

What Your Church Can Do

One day in the Midwest, I happened to run into a man I had known as a pastor years before. At that time he was living in another state.

"Can we have dinner together?" he asked.

That evening I met with him and had a time of fellowship, but what he told me was distressing.

"You know, of course," he said, "that during my last pastorate my wife left me, and we got a divorce."

Then he went on to say that although he had many close friends who were pastors, not one of them showed any concern or wrote him expressing sympathy. He acknowledged that he had not been perfect himself, but his wife, unknown to him, had been having an affair with another man whom she ran away to marry.

My friend cried as he told me that of all the evangelical pastors he knew, most of them wrote hostile letters telling him how wrong he was and that God would surely punish him. "Even to this day," he said, "not one has ever contacted me to say he was sorry for the terrible tragedy that had come to me."

Sometimes fellow Christians can seem cruel and uncaring—an army killing its own soldiers! But is this the way it should be?

Of course not. We read in God's Word: "Come to Me, all you who labor and are heavy laden, and I will give you rest"

(Matt. 11:28). Christians in the church are in a strategic position to understand and to serve people in Christ's name.

In the past, many evangelical Christians felt that it was their job to get people saved, to teach them the Scriptures, and to show them what they should and should not do. But they often left the job of helping people who were hurting to nonspiritual, non-Christians.

Today, attitudes are changing. Many evangelical Christians realize that it is their job not only to evangelize and teach but also to reach out to others who are in special need. It is not unusual to see churches and other Christian organizations helping people around the world.

Local churches can be tremendously helpful to families with problems. Their valuable contributions in some of the following areas can make a big difference in the lives of many people.

An Information Committee

Someone has said that churches are great at forming committees, although some of the committees formed aren't always great! This committee on family problems, however, could be extremely beneficial to the congregation as well as the local community. Its function would be to study family problems, gather information about them, and then serve as a resource to the pastor and church. The group doesn't need to be large, but it should include men and women, a young person (high school or college age), and perhaps a church staff member.

Many fine books, films, and cassette tapes on the family are available. These materials can offer preventive help as well as solutions to existing problems.

Placing a book table in the church is one practical approach in promoting materials. Displaying books on the family in the church library and on bulletin boards is another. Cassette tapes can also be featured.

Setting aside services for showing films on the family is a practical idea. In larger churches adult Sunday school classes can utilize an occasional meeting to show appropriate films, video tapes, and cassettes.

Christian Counseling Services and Related Programs

Some churches across the United States have already recognized the needs of troubled families and the value of professional Christian counseling for them. As a result, some larger churches now offer their own counseling services. Others make frequent referrals to local or nearby clinics.

One problem of a church maintaining its own clinic is securing licensed personnel. Another problem is that most psychologists and psychiatrists specialize in only one or a few types of problems. Consequently, a church with a counselor or two may not be able to offer services for all types of problems in the church. But in a local clinic where several professionals practice together, nearly all types of problems can be treated.

Some church members prefer going outside the local church for private counseling. However, a church can usually make a real contribution by having lay counselors. Such men and women can be trained to handle less severe problems, then refer more complex problems to professionals.

Many churches have joined with other churches to form community centers. Some have formed antiabortion clinics or family planning programs. A few churches have felt the need for youth homes or wife and child abuse shelters, and they have notified local police departments of the availability of these facilities.

Your church can learn how to start programs like these by

contacting other churches, especially large ones that have such ministries. Ask them how they got started and how they keep going. They would be happy to share their knowledge with you and offer suggestions.

After making a study of the established centers, your church should develop a workable plan. Examine your community's needs and what can be done to meet them. With the problems facing families today, churches cannot afford *not* to get involved.

Lectures and Seminars

Some churches arrange to have one seminar a year on family problems. They may encourage members to attend seminars being held in their community or in nearby cities. In this way people can gain insights from specialists and strengthen their families.

Referral List

Most people with family problems don't know where to turn. A family in your congregation may be in need of immediate help but not know where to go. Yet even churches that are not equipped to offer specific kinds of help can furnish referrals. Churches should keep a list of various organizations located in their community, in nearby cities, and across the nation.

Many cities have organizations that have trained professionals and fine facilities. Some national organizations provide counselors, doctors, and shelters. (Some of these are noted in the chapter, "Where to Turn.")

"Peace Lines"

So often a person in trouble needs someone to talk to or advice on which way to turn. Many times such a person will call a church. How tragic when no answer is available for them!

Every church should be thankful for calls requesting help. In a world where most people believe God to be nonexistent or uninvolved, such opportunities to show otherwise would be especially helpful. By establishing telephone lines, churches can show that God and His people care by meeting an immediate need. A church offering an emergency phone line can literally make peace only a phone call away for many people.

A Community Catalyst

One very important service a church and its pastor can render in the area of family problems is to be a catalyst for the community. Often many of the various agencies and service providers involved in a particular case will have different philosophies about what should be done and how to approach the problem. At times the communication between the groups is poor or even nonexistent. At this point a knowledgeable pastor and a caring church can function very effectively as catalysts and facilitators.

A noted authority in the field of child abuse points out that agencies and service providers, despite the increasing awareness of sexual abuse, often fail to recognize the problem and insensitivity in handling the families. School authorities, lawyers, doctors, police officers, and welfare people alike have trouble in interviewing and/or examining the young victims.

The legal system, in an adversarial way, often works for the protection of the perpetrators' rights, sometimes to the detriment of the victims. Schools are frequently caught between conflicting political pressures that all but tie their hands. Because of the conflicting pressures and interests, the end result is stalemate and procrastination. These delays and conflicts of interest are stressful and costly to the particular families involved, to say nothing of the victims.

If a pastor and a church show genuine interest and establish credibility, they can help build effective relationships between the agencies. The pastor can serve as a channel through which communication can flow. There is also a need to monitor the best interests and welfare of the victims.

When hearings are pending, temporary custody and foster care of small children can often be given to the pastor or to someone in the church. The authorities are usually more than willing to consider such a suggestion, and anxious parents can be somewhat comforted and reassured by knowing that their children will receive Christian care.

A young couple's small child was accidentally scalded after the father was assigned to a new location. The authorities automatically assumed child abuse pending investigation and placed the child in foster care. The pastor of the church where they attended was granted foster care responsibility for the child. The concerned parents were able to visit the child daily, yet the courts were assured that she was in good hands. The case was resolved with a minimum of trauma to both the child and the parents.

Another example involved the intervention by a pastor on behalf of a young teen-ager who had been incarcerated after being charged with incest involving his sister. While a plan was being worked out to deal with the problem, his life became endangered by inmates in the jail. They boy was too frightened to report it to authorities but shared it with the pastor. The pastor who was held in high esteem by the sheriff's office, was able to correct the situation at once. The pastor was also able to mediate an equitable solution to the problem that was in the best interest of all the members of the family.

Another vital service that pastors and churches can render is to be aware of the welfare of foster children placed in their community. Most foster parents are above reproach, but some are not. The pastor and parishioners may become aware of cases of abuse and neglect in foster care situations and should report them. They can also serve as reliable reference sources for foster care applicants and help weed out those who might be child abusers.

One pastor was able to render valuable assistance during a hearing a number of times as an *amicus curiae* (friend of the court). If a viable relationship has been established, the judge will often receive a pastor under clergy immunity and permit him to share pertinent and sensitive information in the privacy of the judge's chambers.

Another productive venture in an inner city setting was the practice of recommending selected first-time teen-age offenders to probationary status under the care of the pastor. Most of these youngsters had some connection with the church. In most cases the pastor was able to be quite effective in his influence on the lives of the youngsters and their families.

A word of caution is in order at this point. A pastor and a church should not expect to be accepted as catalysts in the community if they do not show enough concern to establish a working relationship and if they do not do enough homework to be knowledgeable and gain credibility. If they do these things, then their ministry can be most rewarding.

The most logical place in all society to assist families is the church. The pastor, the staff, and every member of the congregation should be alert and willing to help people. One aspect of helping is prevention; the other is solution. A church should offer education and training that will prevent people from developing serious problems, but it should also provide help for those who are already trapped in difficulties.

In the sixth chapter of Galatians, God tells us so much about reaching out and helping other people. Almost every verse is filled with godly instruction about assisting our fellow man: "bear one another's burdens, and so fulfill the law of Christ" (v.2); "Therefore, as we have opportunity, let us do good to all, especially to those who are of the household of faith" (v. 10).

Not long ago I spoke in a church that was geared toward evangelism as well as helping the body of Christ. While talking with the pastor in his office, I glanced in a nearby room that contained shelves of groceries. When I asked him about it, he said, "We continually make our rounds of the supermarkets in this area and ask them to donate their dented cans of food. Of course, we have many other items and any family can take what it needs."

In the evening service the assistant pastor announced to the congregation that if anyone in the church was unemployed, he or she should come to the church on Monday morning and the church would try to find a job for them. The whole church demonstrated a loving concern for people. This same spirit is desperately needed in all churches. It will not only help people with their problems, but it will also bring unusual joy to every member!

Recent years have ushered in many devastating problems, and the family is being fragmented and weakened. But many creative ministries are working to help people at their point of need. As we do this, God will use us to bring healing to many families, and the positive effects on our society will be felt both now and in the future.

The Family in the Years Ahead

One spring day in 1983 I received a call from Washington, D.C., saying that Attorney General William French Smith was selecting a task force to study the problem of family violence, and I was invited to serve on the committee along with eight others.

After completing the call, I wondered whether I was using good judgment in accepting the invitation. What if I should need to attend hearings in various cities at the same time we were offering a week's seminar on our own campus? What if the time of the hearings should conflict with some of my scheduled speaking engagements? Well, I reasoned, if God is in this, He'll work out any conflicts. And so He did.

Lois Haight Herrington, assistant attorney general, led the task force.

The other members were William L. Hart, chief of police in Detroit, Michigan; John Ashcroft, attorney general for the state of Missouri, now governor; Ann Wolbert Burgess, Van Ameringen Professor of Nursing at the University of Pennsylvania and Associate Director of Nursing, Research Health and Hospitals, Boston, Massachusetts. She is also a frequent instructor at the FBI Academy in Quantico, Virginia; Ursula Meese, executive director of the William Moss Institute, a center founded to study and provide information on issues and trends affecting family and life in the future. She is also a member of the Monitoring Board of UNESCO and a delegate of the United Nations Commission on the Status of Women; Ruben B. Ortega, chief of police in Phoenix, Arizona; Newman Flanagan, district attorney of Suffolk County (Boston), Massachusetts; Catherine Milton, an assistant to the president of Stanford University; and Frances Lowery Seward, former director of the Jamaica Services Program for Older Adults, Inc. in New York and secretary of the Victims of Crime Advocacy League.

Our challenge was to gain as much information as possible about the problem of family violence, report our findings to the attorney general, and make recommendations. Our job took exactly one year. In September of 1984, we presented our findings and recommendations to the attorney general in printed form at a ceremony at his office, and we were honored at a luncheon at the White House. The book is available from the Attorney General's office, Washington, D.C.

I must say that the year's work was highly educational and better than getting a second doctor's degree. I feel that the experience was an exceptional opportunity for me to serve my country and to help improve the quality of life in our nation's families.

The testimonies we heard presented by more than one thousand research specialists, victims, and organizations and individuals offering services and shelter to victims of abuse told us about the extent of the problem. As a believer in the Lord Jesus Christ, I sought to be alert to any biblical and Christian aspects. My work in education, psychology, counseling, and family life prepared me somewhat for our overall findings, yet the individual details were often painful to hear.

The day our task force completed its work a man asked me, "Well, what do you think?" I must touch on several points to answer that question.

First, our great nation is blessed with the unparalleled resources of its people. Many competent, knowledgeable people are willing to give of their time and talents in coping with our families' problems.

If there is such a phenomenon as a negative "in thing," family violence (in all its forms) is it. The problem is nationwide; neither rural Alaska nor urban New York is immune. Recently, an intense interest in the problem has become evident. For years the problem was kept hidden on almost all fronts, but now federal marshalls, barbers, waitresses, talk shows, magazines, and other media are openly discussing it.

As you know from our discussions earlier in this book, various emotional, physical, and spiritual causes contribute to family problems. Those multiple reasons complicate the problems and their solutions, but we must look in several directions—not just one.

The average person is sadly lacking in understanding about child abuse, wife abuse, husband abuse, and other aspects of family violence. I think this is only natural. Until recently, who has been talking about it? How many ministers choose to talk about family violence? Too many groups try not to confront the situation, and by their silence they contribute to our general lack of understanding of the problem.

Both lay people and professionals need instruction about family problems and violence. Adult victims see the problem mostly from their devastating, but limited, point of view. They are in the middle of a terrible problem, and they surely understand what they are experiencing. But what of the causes? That may be a different thing. Most of us, including professionals, have tunnel vision about most matters, and it is only natural that a wide range of causes is not understood by most people. A little education in these matters can go a long way toward solving an existing problem or offering preventive help before it gets started.

The great complexity of family violence cannot be over-emphasized, and the problem is far-reaching in its scope. For instance, in some states, if a woman signs a statement against her husband, she is required by law to go through with the complaint and appear in court. She cannot bow out. Say that this woman appearing in court has one infant and one toddler. Should the courts or the state provide child care for her children, since she is legally forced to appear in court to give testimony against her husband? This is only one detail of hundreds.

Our criminal justice system can sometimes be awkward and ineffective and very unfair in its handling of cases involving the family. But during the task force hearings, I was heartened to learn of many people in the system who are trying to cut the red tape, look at the situations realistically, and make sweeping changes.

The shocking incidence of abuse of the elderly, who are often unwilling to report such abuse, demands our immediate attention. Too little action has been taken to this point for their benefit, and the task force's findings clarified the extent of this neglect.

As a licensed psychologist, and as one who has worked extensively in the public schools in the past, I have been aware of the never-healing types of scars that violence leaves on people, especially children in their developing years. My experience on the task force deepened that understanding. No amount of money can ever erase the damage done to a young person who has been continually abused during his "soft cement" years. However, as more people have become aware of the problem, more people have been willing to take steps to stop or prevent such abuse.

Looking to the years ahead I can foresee a potential problem in the whole area of reducing abuse in the family. It has to do with overstepping legal bounds. I can see innocent parents, for example, being erroneously accused of abuse of their children. Any time new laws are passed to correct problems of the past, a period of adjustment is required, and I am sure these laws will be no exception. People in positions of enforcing the law will have to be particularly careful in handling these cases. Some cases have already occurred. I know a Christian family that was "reported" by a neighbor for abusing their child. Actually the parents were not abusing their child, but spanking him occasionally for misbehaving. The authorities called on the home and took the child away. It cost these parents many dollars to employ attorneys, fight the case, and finally get their child back, and the emotional costs of the event were overwhelming for the whole family.

I heard very little spiritual content in the testimonies. It's amazing how people can talk about abuse for months and never mention God or Jesus Christ or the sinful nature of human beings. Being saved, having a new nature, and growing in the Lord don't seem to be realities for many people. Naturally, lack of spiritual understanding cuts out the biggest piece of the pie. We need it if we are going to get at some of the main roots and main solutions to problems in the home.

So, what do I think? I think our nation's families face many problems. We cannot stick our heads in the sand and ignore this reality. To do so would be shirking our duties as citizens and as Christians. We must act responsibly in finding solutions for these problems, and I think we as a nation are dedicated to doing just that.

To this point, many of us may have put these problems in the category of the small brushfire. That is, they occur rather sporadically, and the damage they inflict is restricted in area. Now, more of us are beginning to realize that what we may be facing is a wildfire blazing out of control, engulfing everything in its path. Our job is to put it out; we cannot sit back and hope that it burns itself out.

Foresters have a three-part program of fire prevention, fire detection, and fire fighting. We would do well to learn from them and apply these same measures to family problems. We will have to fight social fires less often if we prevent their causes or detect them in time before they spread.

When we are confronted by problems, we must look to God as our foremost Counselor, but God usually uses people to bring about solutions. I know that the ideas we have discussed in this book can help families prevent and detect many problems related to their well-being. Why am I so certain of this? Because in my years of experience as a family conselor I have seen these ideas work.

Albert Schweitzer said, "The final decision as to what the future of a society shall be depends not on how near its organization is to perfection, but on the degree of worthiness in its individual members." The responsibility for developing those worthy members rests squarely upon the shoulders of the parents in each family. My fervent prayer is that each family will achieve its fullest potential as a healthy family so that the individual members may achieve their fullest potential as worthy human beings, beloved by God and His Son.

Reader Helps

Other books by Dr. Narramore include:
Counseling with Youth
Young Only Once
How to Tell Your Children about Sex
Encyclopedia of Psychological Problems
Life and Love
This Way to Happiness

A Woman's World
The Psychology of Counseling
How to Handle Pressure (coauthored with his wife Ruth)
How to Succeed in Family Living: "The Best of Narramore"

Cassettes by Dr. Narramore include:

T-1 and T-2: You Can Shape Your Future; Study Shortcuts and Success

T-3 and T-4: Choosing Your Life's Work; Marriage: Looking Before Leaping

G-1: The Healing of Your Memories

G-2: The Greatest Thought That Can Occupy the Human Mind

N-1: Understanding Why I Feel and Act the Way I Do

N-2: Humility and a Healthy Self-image; A Visit with the Narramore Family

B-2: The Secret of Being Especially Blessed

G-3: Eliminating Roadblocks to Good Relationships

The Narramore Christian Foundation holds conferences on its campus throughout the year on topics that have been discussed in this book. For information on these conferences write to:

The Narramore Christian Foundation
PO Box 5000
Rosemead, California 91770-0950
(818) 288-7000